The Basic
Patterns
of Plot

FOSTER–HARRIS

NORMAN : UNIVERSITY OF OKLAHOMA PRESS

By Foster-Harris

The Basic Formulas of Fiction (Norman, 1944)
The Look of the Old West (New York, 1955)
The Basic Patterns of Plot (Norman, 1959)

LIBRARY OF CONGRESS CATALOG CARD NUMBER: 59–7493

Copyright 1959 by the University of Oklahoma Press, Publishing Division of the University. Composed and printed at Norman, Oklahoma, U.S.A., by the University of Oklahoma Press. First edition.

To My Dad,

Who loved the far places . . .
Never had much luck but he never quit trying.

Foreword

FICTIONEERING IS THE ART of dreaming visibly by day. A fiction story is a day-dream. As such, it incorporates at least as much of the science of the oculist as it does the opposite seeing of the artist. There are definite and demonstrable techniques—*viewpoint, decision point, reversal,* and the like—which are obviously optics. These techniques can be learned.

There is as much difference between being able to write an acceptable story and showing someone else how to do it as there is between having a disease and knowing how to cure it. And generally, as with medicine, the patient is his own poorest physician. Having first suffered the writing fever myself, with fair results, I have now spent better (or worse!) than twenty years trying to show others how to sell also—again with a record of which I am not in the least ashamed.

For my sins, which must have been as Scarlett's, I have read some thousands of beginners' manuscripts. Their overwhelming faults have been (1) lack of technique, and (2) plain ignorance of what a story is. But these you can learn.

The ultimate message you may have for your readers is yours alone, and nobody may honestly put that in your mouth. But—just as with using the modern dial telephone —the technique for getting in touch with your customer, the ritual of dialing, you may neither ignore nor appreciably alter.

This book concerns itself with the techniques of dialing the reader. What you have to say to him after getting your party is your own affair. Here, though, is what you have to do to call him up.

FOSTER-HARRIS

Norman, Oklahoma
May 14, 1959

Contents

The Basic
Patterns
of Plot

CHAPTER I

The Physiology of Fiction

"In the beginning was the Word," says the Bible. It is the statement of a mystery as great today as when St. John first wrote it. When we begin to read or write, we do start with the word. But what is there about those small marks on paper that give them such magic power? How does the successful author endow them with life? What is the secret of salable writing? In as plain terms as possible, this book will try to help you find out.

The art of writing is at least five thousand years old and it is a craft peculiar to man. No other animal has even begun to communicate by making marks. Something peculiar in man's mental make-up permits and even encourages him to do something unique among living beings. If we could put our finger on what this peculiarity is, we might better understand later just how to turn the trick ourselves. Just what is the secret that makes for successful written communication, for salable writing, either fiction or nonfiction?

Here is its origin. In 1604 the famous astronomer Johannes Kepler deduced from his optical studies that the image on the retina of the human eye must be upside down. In 1625 the Jesuit physicist Christoph Scheiner demonstrated that this was true by observing an excised eye, one from which the sclerotic and choroid coats had been removed so that he could see inside.

The little figures on the mirror-like retina inside were standing on their heads, inverted, just like the images you see on the ground glass of a portrait camera. It was evident then that everything we see in this world we see topsy-

3

turvy—the head where the feet should be, and the feet on top in place of the head.

By some kind of amazing mental gymnastics the human mind has learned to handle most of these crazily inverted images. It has taught itself to "see" heads where heads should be and feet in the proper position for feet. But no one has evidently realized until now that it has only taught itself to "see" correctly those things which the hands can grasp. Mysteries which we cannot grasp, but only see, we continue to see upside down. And here is the basic fact of human psychology, the physiological foundation for the mysteries of religion, the dividing gate between the conscious and the unconscious.

The living word is like the living being. We know intuitively that it possesses two natures. One is a visible form which we can see. The other is an invisible mystery, life. The closest we can come to seeing this life is when the form moves. But so hypnotized are we by form, so determined that even motion must have some kind of structure, some formation, that it is tremendously difficult for us even to divine the true value we seek, that mysterious motion-life.

But suppose we examine our minds for a moment. We know that every human being mysteriously possesses two intelligences, two natures, two kinds of being—one or the other usually dominant, its mate recessive. Religiously, for two thousand years our Western world has distinguished between these two natures. One is the Saint, and the other the Sinner. One the Saved, and the other the Fallen Man. One deems himself serving God, and the other this world; and as the church fathers observed long ago, each considers the other quite mad.

Modern psychiatrists and psychologists, changing the medieval names but not the establishing fact, have called the one mind the "subconscious," "unconscious," "id," or "animal," and the other mind the "conscious," "rational,"

4

or "ego." They have handled the old duality problem in assorted ways and have met with considerable success in special areas. But not one whom I have ever read has stated the basic fact of the *reversal* which establishes human psychology and human problems, the very materials about which we, as writers, must write and plot.

So here it is, as baldly as I know how to put it into words. Here is the essence of literature and literary plot. All proper stories are examples, or copybook illustrations, trying to teach us how to employ reversal—how to get from the inside mind to the outside one, or vice versa.

There are two intelligences, or two kinds of being, in every living human, simply, and self-evidently because eye-equipped, seeing man evolved from simple forms which did not have eyes and which accordingly learned all they knew only from what they could feel.

The simple one-celled animal, the amoeba, for example, had lived in this world for at least one billion years before any creature developed eyes. If you watch a living amoeba under a microscope, you will realize that he is an intelligent little creature. He responds to all sorts of stimuli and even initiates actions of his own. Something inside that little speck of jelly thinks, but examine him as you may you will not find anything even resembling a brain. Evidently all of him thinks in terms of feeling; and you are face to face with the Great Mystery.

About five hundred million years ago the living creatures began to develop eyes. Now the characteristic of an eye is that it operates in exactly the opposite fashion from touch, or the hand. The hand, or the little amoeba with his outer feeling surface, can know only that with which it is actually in contact, that which it touches or grasps. But the eye cannot see anything actually in contact with it, or, indeed, ordinarily any closer than five or six inches. Furthermore, the eye sees what it sees upside down.

Developing eyes, the living creatures of this world by no means jettisoned their amoeba intelligence. Instead, they merely overlaid the primitive contact-mind with a new, visual, events-reported-from-a-distance intelligence. And even we enormously superior human beings, Homo sapiens, continue in exactly this dual pattern. We are made up of a vast complex of simple cells, each possessing a contact intelligence of its own. The body, in other words, is something like a true democracy, with even the lowliest cell the full equal of the highest. Everybody's vote is the same. But over this democratic assembly has been cast a mantle of divine right, a literal neopallium created for, and dictated to by, the eye. This new dictator—to repeat—"sees" everything from exactly the opposite orientation from that by which the democratic cells "feel."

So here is the cross which every human being must bear through life, and here again is our problem.

We live inside ourselves, in the invisible world. But the word, and particularly the printed word from which we seek results, is outside in the visual world. To get the value from outside to inside, or inside out, we must somehow teach ourselves to invert. It is a simple, but enormously difficult, thing to do.

Yet if you will examine any conceivable human problem and the way it was solved, you will discover that this reversal holds true. Here is what writing is trying to tell: *the answer to any possible problem or question you could pose is always in some fantastic manner the diametric reversal of the question.*

Trying to reach the East Indies, Columbus sailed west and so attained enormous and wholly unexpected results. Gutenberg realized that to have fixed print one must start with movable reversed letters. There had been just such reverse symbols on signet seals attached to documents for thousands of years, but until then no one had ever been smart enough simply to see the connection with writing. After the American Revolution, government from the top was replaced, at least in theory, by government from the bottom, and everybody considered it an unheard-of thing. The British bands at the Yorktown surrender played mournfully "The World Turned Upside Down." It took Pasteur to see that dead germs may save you from live ones. In the smallest thing we know, the atom, modern scientists find the greatest power. And in these, and in innumerable other examples, always, always the inversion pattern is evident; the great truth of reversal applies.

Now this has been sensed, if not seen, by men for ages. It is the heart theme of the great religions. Above all, it is the essence of Christianity, it is the secret of sacrifice, and it is supremely exemplified in the whole life of Christ. It is the secret of fiction, of the tales told by the makers of literature of all ages and all nations. It is as simple as that.

I cannot pretend that the mere telling of this will permit you to grasp it. Undoubtedly, in some application you have already practiced the great pattern we are talking about here, and you will probably agree that it was very hard to master. In touch typewriting, for a common example, you will recall, if you have mastered the art, that it took months of energetic practice, and further that perhaps the hardest of all the rules to obey was the one requiring you not to look at the keyboard, but instead at the copy.

It did not seem to make any sense at all, did it, this strange demand that you take not even one peep at what you were doing? Yet, once you learned the trick, once you let the inner Adam with his blind sure sense of place and direction take command of your fingers, why then you began to type much faster and more accurately than ever you could with any seeing hunt-and-peck system.

Any other skill you may possess is of the same order. By long effort and practice, and by the unwitting—at least in most cases unrealized—mastery of the principle of reversal as applied in some particular instance, you have turned words into power, objective things into subjective ability. Now again, this is what fiction is really about, this is its vitamin content, its real food value. It is basically why we read fiction. So, to try to see the principle, and learn to apply it, we shall study it here in its purest and most concentrated form: fictional plotting. The idea is good anywhere, I will assert baldly, leaving you to agree or disagree after you have read what I have to say. But for the student who wishes to learn how to write salable words, both fiction and nonfiction, I can present evidence aplenty. Over a period of some twenty years students and graduates of our professional writing courses at the University of Oklahoma, using these principles, have sold literally thousands of manuscripts to markets from top to bottom, and not only in the United States but all over the world.

With a definite idea of what they were trying to do, making conscious effort toward a goal, quite understandably they arrived much faster than students of equal, or even superior, ability, who strive blindly to learn to sell. And about this also I can testify from experience, because I had to learn both ways.

I found no one to teach me the craft when I decided to try to be a fiction writer. It was some years after I had started selling regularly before I even knew another selling author. What I learned I learned subconsciously first; and it was only after other would-be authors began to show up on my doorstep with hopeful—and generally awful—manuscripts, that I began to see in their writing what I was doing, both correctly and incorrectly, in my own.

Even then it took me some years to learn to express myself in terms the beginner could understand. As I soon discovered, simplicities that seemed plain as day to me were completely invisible to my patients—I think I should call them that, since patience, even more than studiousness, was the necessary quality every one of the eventually successful writers possessed.

I mean what happened to my students was much more what takes place when you go to see a doctor, than when you go to an orthodox teacher.

Probably I have learned more from my students than they from me. I learned early, for one thing, that good teaching is the exact reverse of good personal doing, and accordingly the best performer very seldom can teach much, except by example and implication, while the best teacher is almost never a top performer as well.

Listening to successful performers may bring you a few useful tips and assorted minutiae. But if you expect to learn the real secret of their success, invariably you are disappointed. I think I can say this authoritatively, since I have been listening to scores of successful writers and editors trying—or not trying, as many of them do—to tell others how they did it. Almost without exception they did not communicate with their audiences, simply because, in effect, they were speaking a foreign language.

They themselves had succeeded in terms of *how*, in nuances of delicate rhythms, adjustment of viewpoint, peculiar temperament, and so on. But the majority of them did not consciously know this. They were like the famous Blind Tom, who could play the piano beautifully, even though he had had no training whatsoever, and had no idea how he did it. He knew *how*, intuitively and irrationally. But the listeners were expecting rational terms of *what*.

I remember one wistful lady would-be writer who had just listened to a brilliant writer-editor (this combination is quite rare) give what I had considered a remarkably lucid and simple lecture on story-plot. The lady had taken copious notes and was all aglow.

"I know now what Ive been doing wrong!" she exclaimed

to me. "He said, indent my paragraphs at least an inch, and leave a big margin all around. Then the editors will like to read it! Why didn't you tell me!"

Well, I could have told her to write all she'd learned on the back of a postage stamp and just send that. Then the editors would be even more delighted. But what was the use?

As grim old Galileo observed some centuries ago, there are some numb brains in this world to whom no amount of demonstration will bring enlightenment; and the pity is that no one of us can know ahead whether or not we are in this dumb-bunny classification. The only test is to try.

But, again, after thirty years of trying myself and twenty years of endeavoring to help others try successfully, I am all the more persuaded that even a monkey could learn this trick—provided, that is, that he was a persistent monkey. The secret is not in memory, as with formal education, but instead in seeing for the first time that which you seek, like the hidden faces in a puzzle picture.

You can be absolutely sure that your beginning impressions, memory oriented, are wrong illusions. Your intelligence, similarly oriented to look back and, if possible, connect the past with the present, is likewise of no real value here. Indeed, in my experience, the more intelligent a person is, the more difficult he finds it to grasp this skill. Yet children, completely untutored, regularly tell technically correct stories, and one of the amusing phenomena of our age has been the flood of adult stories told through a child's eyes—having no past to speak of, the child can only see the tale as it should be seen, forward.

Your tall task then, you may be very sure, is to divorce yourself from your deceptive images from the past and to see instead as a child, as one who may enter the kingdom of heaven, yes, and *Saturday Evening Post* and *Cosmopolitan,* and the world of immortal books. This world is timeless. And its realities, hidden beneath the evanescent symbols, are eternal.

This is a very strange doctrine on first impression. It is that reversal exemplified. You are not going to teach yourself something new here. Instead, you are going to unteach your outer self some bad habits. You are going to let your old, inner Adam—who was without sin, remember, because in the Garden, Adam had not yet fallen from God's grace—come out and express himself in this weird, reversed, outer world. Let me say this less metaphysically:

This outer, objective world of images and things may indeed have a complete, separate identity, as science claims. Or it may not, and there is sound argument on this side, too, whether you have ever heard it or not. As we shall notice at greater length presently, science has never been able to find the indivisible unit in matter, the prime building block which surely any complete reality must have. For how can you possibly have a brick house with not one brick in it, or a company, or battalion, or regiment of soldiers consisting entirely of squads, platoons, detachments, but no private soldiers, no individuals? This is the Achilles' heel of present science.

But no matter here. Whether science be right or wrong about the completeness of the outer world, our job here is to add to it. We propose to learn how to let the formless, subjective urge inside of us get out and produce tangible, yes, and salable results in this objective world outside. *We want to create something to sell.*

Very well. We may be very sure, even to begin, that all we have to sell is ourselves, that the sole ingredient of value in our output will be the difference in orientation, the slightly different way in which we see things. Each of us, obviously, does see, or at least may, if we will open our eyes, see from an angle unique with us, not exactly the same as that of anybody else in the world, no, nor of anyone else who ever lived. This different slant is our gold mine. But observe, please, that this is not a tangible thing. It is often very hard to hold. It is a quality, rather than a quantity. Only too frequently we may find ourselves seduced, especially by Pied Pipers with leather lungs and their own devious purposes.

But we must learn to stick to our course, to say it as we see it, even if all the rest of the wide world seems to see otherwise. Which is hard and takes courage. But it is comforting to know that courage is a habit too, which you may plant and cultivate. Now a recap and some beginning ground rules, and we will be ready to start looking at plot by the numbers.

Just as a good fiction story is always a parable, so a correct fictitional plot, the map of the story, must contain a problem, the solution, and the answer.

The answer is always the reverse of the problem.

The method of solution invariably is to invert, to reverse, to "twist" the problem picture so that a new picture abruptly emerges. In the new picture, the answer, again by reversal the seemingly irreconcilable elements of the problem suddenly are reconciled, combined, and unified.

The whole story pattern may be reversed, also. Thus there are three basic ways a story may be correctly plotted:

(1) There is the normal, forward-looking, "happy-ending" story, in which the hero or heroine takes the "right" twist at the climax and so arrives at a plus, or "happy-ending," answer.

(2) There is the normal, forward-looking story, in which the hero or heroine takes the "wrong" turn at the decision point and arrives at a minus, or "unhappy-ending," answer.

(3) Finally, there is the so-called "Literary" or objective story, in which the whole plot is done backwards. This

type of plot begins at the answer, moves back to the climax, decision point, or twist (these are three names for the same thing), and there, since it makes no difference which course the hero elects, either way will take him back to the problem. So, typically, the literary story winds up in futility and unhappiness.

Now this flat statement probably seems like gibberish to you. We shall elaborate presently, with examples. Now for your ground rules:

(A) If you are really serious in your determination to learn to be a selling writer, if you mean business, then you must write a definite minimum amount *every day.* You must make your writing a constant daily habit, *not* an occasional intellectual pastime.

This daily stint need not be much in actual word count. It may vary from one to ten pages, depending upon the individual and how much else he may have to do in his day.

It may interest you to know that the daily output of the average full-time professional writer, at least in my experience, is four to eight finished pages. But notice, I said "finished" pages!

Five times as many words, and as many unfinished, rejected pages, may have passed through the author's typewriter to attain those finished projects. But, as a rule, four to eight pages, or four hours' solid work, is a writer's full day. It requires, incidentally, more real work and more nervous energy to do four hours of creative writing than you would expend in eight hours of ordinary physical labor.

(B) You must strive continuously to write without hesitation, to put down your first thought or first impression. Just as in touch typing, no thinking where the finger should go, no looking down to see! To do so means taking a second thought, correcting that first impulse with a reverse, and all too often perverse, visual impression. Learn not to do it.

You will learn presently, if you persist, that you have

inside you a strange, unerring story instinct, something that guides your plot aright, just as it guides your fingers to the right keys if you are a good typist. Yes, I am saying flatly that I believe story instinct, or plotting ability, is a directional ability, a something which, if not misdirected by local influences, steers you aright with the uncanny ability of a compass.

When you go wrong, as you will, of course, many times, a sort of pressure will begin to build up within you, making it harder and harder to continue. Presently you will come to a dead end. Nothing more will come. But don't be alarmed.

Just back up a bit and try it another direction. If you had the hero entering the room in the preceding paragraph, have him stay outside a bit longer, instead. Change the action arbitrarily, I mean, until something abruptly clicks— as it will. Then go ahead.

With practice, these dead-end side streets and false detours will become fewer and fewer, until eventually you will be able to do almost—but not quite—a correct plot at the first draft. In pulp writing very often this not-quite-right first draft will get by. It almost never does in slicks, and even veteran authors write and rewrite and rewrite again, to get the necessary perfection and polish. Don't be perturbed if you can't do in your first draft what it takes them five or ten revisions to accomplish. That is what polishing means.

(C) Do not show anybody else your copy, and do not discuss your plots with anyone else.

There is an exception here. If you are fortunate enough to have a competent coach, an instructor who knows his business, why then he can be a tremendous help and timesaver. But be sure he is competent before you go too far with him. The test of competency is very simple. If he knows how, he can plot, and you can sense that what he suggests is a plot and does have life. But if he offers only negative suggestions, has only faults to pick and no constructive changes to offer, then probably he is not the coach for you.

You do not need to accept the changes he suggests in your plot, please understand. But he must be able to see and suggest genuine plot improvements, and these you will ordinarily be able to recognize as story. You may feel it is "his" story and not your own. The idea then is to do something similar to his, in your own terms, with your own conceptions of proper characters and actions. Again, if your instructor is competent, he will understand this and accept your changes readily. He is really trying to teach you to add and subtract. If he prefers to add elephants, and you mice, what difference does that make, so long as the addition is correct?

But do not discuss your plot with fellow students, or, worse yet, with casual amateurs. Do not read your copy to anyone save a competent coach. If you would like to see just why, then try putting two compasses together.

Touching, they point to each other, and so become absolutely worthless as directional guides. Human minds tend to do precisely the same thing. Your true reader, you must remember always, is the distant editor and the still more distant magazine or book buyer. Let the editor be your first reader, if you would be a professional; and let the others read what you write in print!

CHAPTER II

Viewpoint

IF YOU HAVE EVER HAD anything to do with land surveying or navigation, or even have learned to read maps, this will come much easier, because here we are going to consider just how a fictional plot is established, a story begun. But even if you lack any of these technical skills, no matter. This is so simple that even a child can master it. Just remember, please, that it is something you must study. You will not get it in one swift reading, no, nor in two, probably, or three, or even four.

A fiction story and the plot which is its essence, its digest, begin, like everything else real in this world, from a specific point.

In land surveying, which we can use for comparison, this point is called a landmark, bench mark, property stake, or corner post. These are all basically the same thing. In an area which has already been surveyed, the surveyor will look for the property stake or corner post established by the previous surveyors, as the point from which to begin his own survey. Land and bench marks usually are public conveniences, located after careful geodetic and astronomical observation by government surveyors. These precise landmarks define the location and boundaries of all real properties in their surveys, and altering or moving a landmark has been a high crime since biblical days. Of course, in a virgin area, a surveyor must establish his own boundary monument, his beginning point, more or less arbitrarily.

Now notice something that often confuses writing students. Once he has found or established his landmark, a land surveyor does not go behind it, does not locate it with reference to some previous point. Instead, by custom and by law, the landmark is declared a prime starting point, immaculately conceived, if you will. No irreverence is intended, let me add hastily. Instead, this simply follows God's own example. To go behind a prime landmark, even if it were permitted, would be only to create endless confusion and chaos.

In savage societies this area behind a prime landmark and the things or actions presumed to be in such an area are taboo, forbidden, while the face of the landmark turned toward the surveyor, the one side he is lawfully permitted to see, is totem. Failure to understand this essential nature of taboo and totem has produced much fuzzy writing by some anthropologists.

In land surveying the surveyor ordinarily sets his transit over the landmark first, beginning there. All succeeding stations are located carefully with basic reference to the landmark, and as the survey is completed, if possible, it "closes," that is, comes back to the point from which it started. Obviously this is not possible in surveying a route for, say, a road or pipeline. But for a farm or county or city subdivision or the like this is what happens.

Now a fictional story and its plot, in their different medium, do precisely the same thing. Just as a surveyor must begin by learning to use a compass, level, and transit, so a student must start by mastering *viewpoint*.

The normal story employs a viewpoint located inside the viewpoint character's mind. This VP, as it is usually abbreviated in writers' jargon, may be the hero or heroine. In the simple story he usually is the main character. But he may be a minor character, a mere bystander who sees the story happen while taking little or no part in it himself. In years past, quite often he was the author in person, frankly interjecting himself into the narration. At least one of our most famous modern authors continues to use this authorial VP device.

The purpose of the VP is to locate, focus, limit, and define the story. Like the surveyor's landmark, he, the VP, is the opening and closing point. Everything is told with direct reference to him, and nothing he cannot see, hear, think, or feel can properly be included in the story.

Let me restate this as simply as I can. The VP character actually is conceived and written in the first person, even though the formal third person may be used throughout the story. But for the VP character all of the details, both public and private, that only "I" would see, hear, think, and know must be set down.

The other characters in the story are drawn in real third person, the natural reflection of the VP first person. That is, they are described only as the VP character sees, hears, thinks, and feels about them. Their private thoughts and feelings (which would be unknown to the VP character, naturally) are not given. Nor can you describe what they do when they are out of the VP character's view. He can hear of their doings, someone can tell him, or he may figure it out for himself. But you must no more put into your story what the other characters do when the VP character is absent, or when they are behind his back, than you would include in a picture of whatever you are looking at now the way the other side of it looks also, or the view at your back.

There is a logical reason for this, as we shall see immediately. But first, the easiest way to learn it is to write your first efforts at plot or story in actual first person, confession-story style.

Call the hero or heroine "me." Now plot or write as "I" would see, hear, think, and feel it. After you have done this, if you wish, you may take your pencil and change all the "I's," "me's," and "my's" to "he's" or "she's" as the gender may be. You will discover that a definite first-person feeling still clings to your VP character, sharply distinguishing him from all the rest.

The king may call himself "Our Majesty," or the learned judge, "The Court," but he still means "I."

Here is the reason for this. It is that reversal principle in action again, and to see it we need an illustration. Imagine yourself looking down a railroad track, seeing where the rails appear to come together at the vanishing point on the horizon.

Now you know with your intellectual overbrain that they do not come together, they are parallel. But no matter how highly educated or how intellectual you may be, your eye stubbornly refuses to see them parallel; your eye continues to report that they do too come together, and right there at the horizon.

This illusion is actually a reversal. There is a genuine physical point where the rails meet. Not out there on the right-of-way in the form of rails, true. Instead, they meet in your eye, in the form of rays of light.

There is a focal point in the lens of your eye where the rays of light do meet and cross over, reversing the outer picture. This point you see reflected in the landscape, in this case in terms of railroad rails. But the vanishing point, seemingly on the horizon, is nothing in the world but the reflection of your own viewpoint, just as you would see your face reflected in the mirror.

But if this be true, and it is (it is the foundation of artistic, pictorial representation), then what would you suspect about the rest of the things you see out there? Are they actually there, or is something throwing back at you a reflection of yourself, just like a looking glass?

You may answer that question for yourself. But you will notice that the form of any object depends almost entirely on the particular angle from which you view it, while the color is also a subjective aspect, painted on by the perceiving eye. There are those persons who see no colors at all, but only black and gray, while many more are color limited, seeing only a part of the glories we more fortunates know.

But take away the form and the color from what you see out there, and what do you have left? This may be a hard one to answer!

Once more, here is another reversal secret. The ingredient of value in the treasured old master is not the Dutch peasant, or pot, or pan, or river, or whatever that painter painted. Instead, the value lies in *how* he painted that whatever or whoever it was, in *how* he saw his world, in *how* he selected and arranged and located for us the facets of his viewpoint, marketing them for us with whatever junk was handy—pots, or Dutch peasants, or tulips, or what have you.

We think we look at a portrait or scene. But instead, really, we are looking through a seeing, we are being permitted to know as he knew the vibrant thrill of a master's living eye. What difference what we, or he, look at, when a man can look like that! And the same also applies to a great story.

Writing, or at least fictional writing, we must not forget, is nothing in the world but the most highly conventionalized form of picture painting. The first written words were pictures, of birds, cows, arrowheads, warriors, the thousand and one things the first would-be writers saw and wished to show—since they could not be there in person to tell—to others. We do not know it now, but even the letters of our alphabet, many of them, began as pictures. The "A," for example, was originally Aleph, an ox, drawn like this: ꝩ. You will notice that before it got down to us, somebody neatly reversed it.

If writing is a form of art, of drawing or painting, then the same general rules should apply. We find that they do. The pictorial artist's use of vanishing point and perspective is nearly reversed in our use of viewpoint and plot. We also know linear perspective, as we shall see in greater detail presently; and we use aerial perspective, chiaroscuro, and foreshortening. We have our equivalent of color and line: with us color words, which convey emotions, and line words, which depict motion and shape.

There are four basic kinds of viewpoint, of which one, intersection, is by far the most important. The kinds of VP are *radiation, traversing, intersection,* and *resection.*

Radiation is the sort of diction we may expect to hear when the VP character stands put and describes the scene about him, locates himself, or perhaps exhorts, poetizes, or prays. A typical example might run about like this:

> I stand in the center of the great square. In front of me is the City Hall. To my right is the civic park and to my left the First National Bank building. Before me is the main avenue of the city. . . .

Note, in this form of VP the character does not move. He does not cross motion or form words with emotional words. He merely locates and describes; and then sometimes he adds an appeal to the previously located entity or entities, or asks a reaction from the reader, presumably looking out through the VP character's eyes.

The Lord's Prayer is another example: "Our Father [identification], who art in heaven [location], hallowed be Thy Name [exhortation]," and so on.

Traversing. This form of viewpoint describes the VP character in motion. It is the sort of thing you find typically in travelogues, guidebooks, accounts of journeys, and the like. It does not exhort, and it locates only in a linear fashion, like stringing beads on a thread. A fair example is:

> Tuesday we spent in San Antonio. The next day we drove to Dallas, a distance of some 270 miles. Thursday we went on to Oklahoma City . . . .

Observe that the VP character is saying "we" in this example, but, plainly "I," that is, the VP character in his own first person, must have been along. Had the example said "they," then the VP character would have to be telling someone what he had learned about "their" journey: "They told me they spent Tuesday in San Antonio," etc. The point to remember is, always stick with the VP character and write of *his* actions, *his* thoughts, *his* emotions, *his* speeches. Do *not* write primarily the effect of what he may be thinking or speaking about. In this example—*"They told me,"* of what "I learned," or "I knew"—the objective fact is secondary.

Intersection. This is by far the most important and generally used type of viewpoint, and it is the one on which you should concentrate. It also uses a surveying and pictorial art technique, that of exact location of points, or "where the lines cross." An example first before we analyze:

> *Thrilled to the core,* I stood for a moment at the sagging gate. *I was home.* I took a step forward, *swallowing at a huge lump in my throat.* Morning sunlight streamed *gloriously* across the *dear, worn, old* porch, and the door was opening. *Mother* was coming out, *surprise,* and then *joy flashing* across her face. "John, *darling!*" She flung herself toward me.

The technique here is to imagine oneself inside the VP character, aware of his most private emotion. Set this down. It is the part italicized in the example. Then imagine oneself moving quickly outside of the VP character, to see what he does as he experiences the emotion. This is the part not italicized. Now cross the two impressions. "Thrilled" [the emotion], "I stood" [the fact or motion], and you have an exact definition, a precise location of a point in your story. In land surveying, pictorial art, and fictional writing, a point is located and created by intersecting lines; and in fiction writ-

22

ing these lines are drawn from the opposite ends of the base line of reality, from the subjective and objective extremes.

Before I go further, let me make one aspect clear. This is also a rhythm which we are creating with our emotion-motion, emotion-motion succession. Here is another of the prime secrets of good fiction, and one that your English teacher possibly didn't tell you, so don't skip this paragraph. There are both words and music in a good story, just as in a song; and in fiction, as in music, the tune is more important than the words.

The "music" of fiction is the emotion-motion, emotion-motion, up-and-down beat, or, if you prefer, the feeling-fact, feeling-fact rhythm. As in music, the emotional parts are upbeats, the motion or fact portions downbeats. Let me make it clear also that I do not mean good fictional writing is tom-tom stuff, mechanically and without variation feeling-fact, feeling-fact, feeling-fact.

On the contrary, the score varies like that of a good tune. You can score a piece of competent fictional writing. You will come up with something that reads like this: feeling-fact, feeling-fact, feeling, feeling, fact, fact, feeling-fact, feeling-fact, feeling-fact, fact, fact. And so on. It is more subtle than the meter of poetry, more intangible than the notes of music, but of the same order and for the same purpose.

Beat, rhythm, and vibration are the tangible evidences of life. They are how you put life and vitality into otherwise lifeless words, describing objective things, mechanical actions. Now let's look at this from the draftsman's angle and see how we do it on paper.

When a land surveyor starts to map an area, he begins typically by running a base line from his landmark or corner post. Then each succeeding point is located by intersection, that is, by holding the rod on the point and "shooting it in," taking precise observations from each end of the base line. Where the lines of sight cross on the mapping paper the point "is at," exactly located. The whole complex of the survey map is built up of these points, like a building, brick by brick. This is what we do also in fiction.

We paint a picture, point by point, exactly locating each point by shooting it in from the subjective and objective ends of our base line. We remember that a subjective line uncrossed by any line of action or fact has no point established on it, and neither does an objective line which is not intersected by a subjective line. We paint this way because it is the way our eyes, and our eye-shaped minds behind them, work, because it is the way our brains "see."

Looking at something, your eyes locate it by triangulation, where the line of sight from one eye crosses the line of sight from the other. Each eye individually has also a range-finding mechanism, something like that of the military range finders. Each eye, I mean, records at least one erect and two inverted images of anything at which it looks; and we may feel quite sure it must use them as does the military range finder, carefully matching the inverted to the erect image in a point of coincidence, and thus establishing a basis for calculating the range.

Both eyes together, however, are much more accurate in locating and determining the distance to any object within the limits of stereoscopic vision, which is approximately 480 yards for the unaided eyes. Now here is why I am telling you all this:

All we know, all we shall ever know, of anything in this world is: (a) where it is "at," with reference to ourselves, and (b) in some few instances what to do with it should we be able to grasp it. The first is intellectual knowledge, mainly memory, and the second, subjective skill.

This may sound startling, I know, this reduction of the seemingly vast fields of human knowledge to such bare

24

simplicities. But consider an example before you refuse to believe.

Suppose we want to know what the word *canine* means. Well, we know where "at" to look—in the dictionary, which is "over there." In the dictionary we also know where "at" to turn, under "C." We find that *canine* means "dog."

Now, "dog" is already in our scheme of things, because we know what that is. Rather, we know *where* he is—mine is over yonder by the sofa, asleep on the rug just now—not one of us can honestly say we know *what* he is. My own dog, again for example, has sometimes been mistaken for a door mat. But in our scheme of things, our personal map of reality, we can ordinarily distinguish a dog from, say, a cat or an elephant, and perhaps we can even tell different dogs apart. Really we simply know where the point "dog" is "at," and we can tell one dog point from another. That is our intellectual knowledge, *in toto*.

But subjectively we may also have the ability to train dogs, to teach them to hunt, or catch rodents, or act as watch-dogs and guides. This ability is skill, something very, very different from intellectual knowledge. We should take care never to confuse the two, although we often do.

Skill, however, is not something which can be reduced to words. The mere purchase of a book on dog training does not make you a good dog trainer. Similarly, the mere purchasing and reading of this book will not automatically make you a competent fiction writer, alas! Instead, you must practice the principles set down here, do them yourself, try and try and try again, until at long last your inner man grasps what the outer intelligence sees and wants him to do.

And viewpoint is the first essential your inner man must grasp and learn to exercise. Viewpoint is the seed of plot; it contains within itself all you will need to know to plot and write correct, salable fiction. Believe me, this is so! The next chapter, on the structure of the normal plot, will show you how this works. But first, here is something for you to do:

Practice writing in viewpoint until you are sure, very sure, that you know what it is and can do it, can stay in VP!

Write in first person, changing the "I's" to "he's" or "she's" only after you have finished. Notice carefully how that first person limits and focuses the field of view, how it selects this (in front of the VP character, where he'd be bound to see it) and rejects that (behind him, or around the corner, where he couldn't see it). Try to realize that you are *not* writing about the things, people, and actions out there at all, but instead of *how* a living "I" would see them, how it would sort and select and arrange them in its own distinctive and individual pattern.

Note, if you will, that the First Commandment is also a rule for writers: "Thou shalt have no other gods before me." If that does not establish the primacy of the first person, "me," of the subjective, and of the Indwelling God who is within us all, and who urges us constantly to creative expression, then I cannot read plain English.

I have deliberately omitted a description of the fourth kind of viewpoint, *resection*, here. This is the currently used, so-called "literary," viewpoint. It is sometimes mistakenly identified as omniscient viewpoint, that is, the view of the Lord. Patently it is no such thing, for the Lord assuredly sees and knows everything at once, which is an impossibility for a mere human writer, who can see and describe only one view at a time. Resection is simply the objective reversal of ordinary subjective viewpoint and will be described at length in the chapter where it applies, on the literary plot.

CHAPTER III

The Normal Plot

A CHILD WILL LEARN this easily, but, because it is so simple, it may prove—for an adult—very, very hard. We adults learn only the complicated easily. But here, now, is the hidden plot pattern that may be found in the stories of all men, in all ages and places. Always it is basically the same; and the more different it may appear to be superficially, the more orthodox it will ordinarily prove to be on closer analysis. For, as somebody said long before the French, the more things seem to change, the more certain it is that they're the same old thing.

This is entirely understandable, at least to us. We have only to notice that all men, of all ages of which we have any records, looked out on their world through eyes anatomically and optically the same as ours.

They, too, bore our cross. They also faced our riddle of existence, the contradiction between an inner, upright intelligence, depending for its wisdom upon feelings, and an outer, visual intelligence which saw everything in just the inversion, the upside down, of the inner concept.

We know this to be so not only from the mummies of ancient Egypt, from the skulls the archaeologists have found, but also from the art and artifacts which other men have left us, some dating from long, long before the dawn of writing and history.

Story telling and plotting are much older than writing itself. The first tales were told, passed from mouth to mouth, and the singsong of the storyteller, the aural structure of fiction, is still with us. You must listen to a plot, a

27

story, before you can say surely that it is a good story, a correctly balanced plot.

Let me tell you a little about the beginnings of story, and of writing itself, before we go on to the current aspect of the normal plot. In southwestern France and the Spanish peninsula you may still see the work of some of the first plotters, if you wish. These "plots," in the form of drawings on the walls and roofs of caves, are at least ten thousand, and some of them probably twenty-five thousand, years old.

They were drawn, carved, or painted by prehistoric men from the Aurignacian to the Magdalenian periods, a stretch of some fifteen thousand years or more, and they have, for the most part, been rediscovered only within the past fifty years. They have baffled the archaeologists. But if you understand plot, then you know very well that they are not a thing less than prehistoric plotting, the ancestors of story.

These drawings and paintings are found far back in dark caves, in black crevices extraordinarily difficult to reach. Among the very earliest are outlines of human hands against red or black backgrounds. Next come silhouettes of animals, and then beautifully executed paintings of mammoths, rhinoceroses, bears, deer, bison, wild horses, oxen, boars, the fauna of a vanished world. Now add something found all over Europe, the female statues known as the Aurignacian Venuses, and we have a complex as illuminating as it is fascinating.

Twenty thousand years ago these remote ancestors of ours had discovered the enigma that we also know, namely, that man lives in two worlds, an inner and an outer; and it is extraordinarily difficult to get anything from the outside in, or, worse yet, from the inside out.

The medieval astrologer named these two worlds the microcosm, or little, inner world, and the macrocosm, or great, outer creation. We do not know what the Aurignacian artist called them. But, as writers, we may be very sure that we know why he painted what and where he did. We can know this because, for one reason, there are still primitive peoples, the Australian aborigines among them, who paint animal figures on cave walls for magical and religious purposes. And, also, we ourselves know how plot, plan, and story are generated.

A story is first "seen" as a kind of dream, against the black backdrop of our eyelids, in the little world, the microcosm, of our closed eyes. Many writers have testified to this, saying flatly that they do see their stories and characters, that often these inner world visions are more vivid, more realistic, than real life.

Yes, but a story thus "seen," or dreamed, is still a story not yet caught, not reduced to objective form which may be passed out to others, which may be shown in the outer world. So the Aurignacian artist, like ourselves, had the problem of what to do about his dream—how to transfer it from inside his head out into his strange prehistoric world.

He sought darkness for the setting of his drawings for the same simple reason that we associate night with dreaming—how often we discover that a plot we could not, for the life of us, solve the day before is clear as day, complete and ready the next morning, after we have slept on it! Mammoths, buffaloes, horses—these the prehistoric artist needed for his food, for hides for clothing, for bones and horns and tusks, for weapons, tools, and ornaments. He dreamed about them, about slaying or capturing them. What more natural than to try to transmit his dream, give it objective birth, get it out into the objective, waking world!

The pictures of the hunters' prey, and of the traps that caught some of them, are still there, twenty thousand years later, on the dark walls which were the closest approach to the microcosm the artists could find. These were the world's first recorded stories and plots.

The outlined hands we can read, too, because the hand is the eye of the inner intelligence. It is the part which, above all, feels. What more natural than to begin with it? Finally, the little Venuses:

The female is the beginning of form. That is a basic axiom of art. It is why the artist typically begins with her and ends with her; it is the reason for nudes, and the further reason why one nude may honestly be pure art, another carnal error. It depends upon the direction the artist is going —from, or to, his landmark.

The Aurignacian art degenerated at last into queer little geometric markings on pebbles, the *Maz d'Azil* stones, which we can suspect were the first attempts at objective writing. Doubtless, though, these early would-be authors no more knew what they were attempting than does the typical modern amateur. But real writing, as we know it from existing records, originated everywhere in a similar succession. First there were actual pictures of the concepts the writer was trying to convey—birds, oxen, arrows, what-not. Then came more and more conventionalized representation of these pictures, more and more use of homonyms (that is, use of pictures to express words with the same pronunciation but different meanings: a bee, for the verb "be," for instance, or a bear for the act of bearing a burden or baring one's breast). And at long last the alphabet has become completely changed, reversed, and conventionalized.

But the problem remains—the same today as it was in the ice ages, the same so long as the human eye, the human hand, remain unaltered:

How do I transfer a subjective, inner urge or desire into an outer, objective fact or accomplishment?

Closer yet: *I have an inner conflict of emotions, feelings.* (If I am a cave artist, I am hungry, I want to eat the bear, but I am also afraid of him. What shall I do—risk death or go hungry?) *What, in any case, can I do externally to resolve the inner problem?*

Because stories must be told externally, in terms of things and actions, most people never consciously see what is actually being written about. But bear this always in mind. The story actually takes place inside the breast of the character, the hero or heroine experiencing it. What he or she says and does are merely the symptoms, the effects of that inner conflict. We must tell our story in shadows, like those the prisoners in Plato's famous cave saw and considered the real world. But that does not prevent us, the real creators, from really seeing, really knowing what we are doing. We know the true story is always inside.

The *normal plot*, accordingly, will always shape up much like a simple problem in arithmetic—one of addition, the "plus" or "happy-ending" story, or one of subtraction, the "minus," or "unhappy ending." But in place of numbers we substitute emotions.

The basic emotions are very simple. Although stories can be and are written on them, ordinarily we use the conditioned emotions instead, which provide us with well-nigh infinite combinations. Thus, although basically love and hate, attraction and repulsion, may well be considered the fundamental feelings, we can deal also with pride, ambition, honesty, loyalty, hope, patience, wrath, conditioned fears (of falling, for instance, in a plot about a steeple jack, say), courage, lust, greed, and slothfulness—in short a whole panorama of possible antagonists.

We shall find that most stories are written about a very few problems—*pride* versus *love* being a favorite women's story conflict, *honesty* versus *fear* a problem to be found in every western magazine, and *ambition* versus *loyalty* a common general magazine difficulty. For feminine readers nearly always one of the emotions must be love. But, if we are skilled enough, we can write successfully about almost any combination we please.

I am dealing here with the short story, which bears about the same relationship to the longer stories that simple fractions do to complex ones. Certainly any student of plotting would do well to learn the short story first, for these principles, expanded, apply to a novel plot as well.

Now we shall see precisely how a normal short-story plot sets up:

Fear versus *honor* $= ?$

We adopt some conventions here. Just as there certainly are no real lines of force in nature, though Faraday invented them and made them one of the most useful tools of science, there are no plus, minus, or equals signs in the world of natural things either, although we find them tremendously helpful in arithmetic and getting things solved. So our signs here are not objectively real, but instead are just conventions, for our own purposes. I hope this is clearly understood.

If so, we can get ahead with our patterning. We can agree to use a more informative sign than "versus," for one. We can say "plus," or "$+$," for a "happy-ending" story (do you notice that the plus sign is simply another form of the cross?) and "minus," or "$-$," for the "unhappy-ending" story.

The "answer" is another detail that may bother us at the start. Actually we have no word for the real story-answer. It is either a combination of emotions or of reversed emotions that is a true ineffable. We can give it a name, of course. Probably "satisfaction" or "content" or "happiness" would be very close in the "plus" story, and "despair" or "deprivation" or the like would approach the "minus" answer. But we will just stay simple here and use the familiar elementary arithmetic "sum" and "remainder," or just "answer," and let it go at that.

We can try, at least, to remember that in solving a story-plot we are doing, in our poor way, just what Jesus Christ did in supreme fashion, for He also was a storyteller and His parables are short stories. The kingdom of heaven, we are assured by the Bible, is a world of light and joy, an emotion, an enduring contentment. A world not of things and not made with hands. Perhaps, long ago, old Johannes Kepler, the astronomer, was right when he said it could be, in this world, that we are but the servants of a far brighter world we cannot see, a world of light waves and rhythms. At least we know that in a normal, forward short story our main purpose is to leave our reader with a happy, satisfied, enduring emotion.

Back again to our example equation:

Fear + honor = satisfaction.

It begins to sound as if we were writing something biblical, doesn't it? To fear and honor the Lord—but does *fear* in the way it is used in the Scriptures mean "to be afraid of," as we might fear a deadly snake or a vicious burglar?

We know it does not. We know without being told that somehow the ordinary meaning of fear is here reversed into something else, into love and respect. It is the same as when we say we fear our father's or mother's wrath, when we know very well, and so does everyone else, that what we mean is, we love them so deeply that we fear to displease them, and we know that if we do anything to give them displeasure, it will be some foolish thing that will hurt us far more than it does them.

Just so, then, with our emotion, "fear," here. This being a "plus" story, something is going to happen to it to change its usual nature. And once again, let me give some comparative examples.

When a man and woman marry, the woman ordinarily gives up her name, taking that of her husband. And we say the two "have become one." Similarly, though perhaps you never thought of it, having learned your arithmetic so early, in sums the individual factors merge their identities into a new unit. The "one apple" plus "one apple" becomes "two apples," the sum. In some mysterious fashion this sum is not two separate apples as before, but instead a unified answer, one sum, one apple that is somehow twice as big, twice as luscious and bright and tempting as either of the individual apples that went into it. Just so also with our answer here.

But what happens to produce this remarkable result? Well, plainly, some kind of operation does take place at the equals sign. Something strange occurs here. And once again we have arrived at a human phenomenon known to all men and grappled with by virtually all peoples of whom we have any knowledge, because here is the reason and the meaning for religious sacrifice.

In all places and times we find the idea of making sacrifices a part of religion. There have been the burnt offerings of the nations of antiquity, the sacrificial ceremonies performed by the priests of all nations at the altars under every sky, even the horrible perverted sacrifice of children to Moloch. Some deep, universal impulse obviously drove, and still drives, human beings to make this—on first, superficial impression—seemingly utterly senseless gesture. What is it?

It is the necessity for unity and orientation that is a prime requisite of individual human existence—the basic need to have a prime, enduring landmark, a great "one" on one end of the line of reality, a corner post from which all the other things in this world may take location and direction.

The line of reality, we must constantly remember, is always first person singular subjective at one end, third person plural objective at the other.

There is no complete reality in this world, unless some

individual first person is looking at it, hearing it, or feeling it. Conversely, it is impossible to discover a true, individual, indivisible unit, a genuine "one" in the world which our senses can grasp. The atom, once considered to be the prime, indivisible building block, has since turned out to be composed of electrons, protons, and whatnot. The electrons and protons in turn have proved to be electrical charges, "sums," that is, and not true, indivisible unities. Here is the mystery of science.

In the objective world there is no real first person. In the subjective world there are no other persons, save one real "me"! But how do we get from "I" to "them," or vice versa? We say there is a way—reversal or sacrifice.

This tremendous truth we try to make usable to our readers even in the lightest of plots and stories. We do not worry about it, now, mind you! Its purpose is the purpose of God, beyond our comprehension. But it is what Moses knew and used when he led the children of Israel out of Egypt, into the Promised Land. His language was different from ours. What a modern man would, perhaps, say, describing the great event, is that Moses was given a sense of direction, that he was told by God that one cannot have many North Poles in this world and go anywhere accurately and safely.

The Egyptians, sedentary nontravelers, could exist worshiping many gods. They always remained within sight of them. But Moses, traveling the uncharted wilderness, must have one compass, one North Pole, one God to steer his course aright. This is viewpoint, to repeat. Now we consider the element of sacrifice, which arises from viewpoint and of which the whole life of Christ is our supreme example:

If it were physically possible to travel right through the vanishing point and, like Alice in Wonderland, actually reach the marvelous land on the other side, we can be quite certain we would find many things far different from the way we see them in this objective world. Remember, viewpoint actually is the reality of which vanishing point is but the reflection, the mirror image. Once we grasp this, we know some things about that inner world we are trying to reach. We know, for one, that everything in there must be unified, first person singular subjective. And we know from optics and the mechanism of the human eye that everything will be reversed—right will be left; left will be right; up, down, and down, up; and some of those who are here first will there be last; and the cornerstone rejected by the builders here will there be found in its true place, its prime purpose.

So, when our normal, forward plot reaches its Garden of Gethsemane, its "equals" sign, a value of this world must be reversed, "sacrificed." The hero must make a *decision* to do the "right" thing, and he must act upon it. Mere lip service is not enough. Always at this point the "wrong" choice will seem the safe, sane, and sensible one, the "right" course ruinous.

Always here also the sacrifice must be made for the sake of someone else. This is basic! The reason is that we are at the point of a reversal, the great secret, the heart of plotting. We cannot yet see how matters will be on the other side. But we do know they will be the inversion, the reverse of what we see here. Therefore, a righteous sacrifice for others on this side will reverse into a gain for me individually, a reward, on the other side. And I must follow my moral sense of direction, my inner feeling for what is the "right" course and which the left or "wrong" course.

My intellect, the product of my senses, will here lead me wrong unless I am careful. This is why all the church fathers strongly distrusted the evidence of the senses and instead instructed the Christian to follow the way of Christ and to depend on God's grace. By which last we can assume here they meant that inner sense of moral direction which,

36

in some measure, is shared by us all and which comes to us as the magnetic lines of the earth come to and direct the compass.

The compass does not make the directions it points. Instead, without intellectual argument, it humbly obeys the great silent impulses it feels, it points the silent way already in creation.

At the moment of decision and action the hero must not be able to see or reason his way through.

This is merely another way of saying that the decision and action, the "sacrifice," must seemingly be made for someone else. All we can see from this side is in reverse, never forget. And it is the hardest trick in the world intellectually to calculate the exact reverse, the opposite, of what we see. It is the secret of all great discoveries, great inventions. But, almost without exception, it comes without effort; it must be permitted to come to you, and you cannot forcibly catch it. You do not create the lines of force, even those of this world.

The interval of decision and sacrificial action in a plot is ordinarily called the *dark moment*, for obvious reasons.

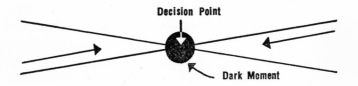

Now what happens? Imagine yourself actually going through the reversal point in the accompanying diagram. There are two things you can do as you approach that point through which you cannot see, but through which you must pass. We will assume that you have chosen to try to guide right, stay on the right hand side of the road, as most people do, though this righteous impulse is by no means universal.

Some people, the Marquis de Sade, for one notorious example, or Aleister Crowley, the devil worshiper, actually deify evil and choose perversely as a matter of course. And what they would do to traffic on a crowded highway, if they put their doctrine into practice there also, as they sometimes do, you can imagine! But most people do have the normally right impulse, and we'll assume you have also.

Your problem is to get through the dark point and there are two possible ways of attempting it. You can try hugging the right-hand curb. In which case, if you succeed, at the decision point you will go crooked and come out, amazingly and perhaps disastrously, on the left-hand side of the road over there. Right and left also reverse at the decision point, notice!

Or you can elect to go straight through, even though from this side that does appear to be the utterly foolhardy course, eminently calculated to throw you right into the face of oncoming traffic, in the perfect spot for a wreck.

This is a normal, "happy-ending" story we are plotting now, remember. You decide to "go straight," accordingly— have you heard that somewhere before?—and you act on it, you "sacrifice yourself," you do go straight through.

And here the "twist" you have heard so much about in stories and plotting operates. What logically and intellectually should have been the left-hand side of the road suddenly becomes the right. Where you were going, in a twinkling you are coming. You have made a reversal and now that you are through it, you can see that it makes sense on the other side, just as things made sense on the other side also, but in a reverse order.

Merely because you are driving south down a road, and keeping to the west side, which is also your right, does not mean that drivers heading north should also cling to the west curb. For them, right is east; and if you would join their line of traffic, you also must reverse your way and match your enduring right to the enduring east now, rather than west. This is difficult only because it is so simple.

Again, what happens when you make the twist, the reversal? We took as an example the plot-problem *fear* + *honor*, a much used and very familiar story basis. Let's clothe it with symbols now, specific characters and actions— which, we will remember, have just as much to do with what we are actually doing as apples have to do with arithmetic. Let's imagine a town marshal in the West, who has just married and is preparing to leave town with his bride on a honeymoon trip. The news comes that a gang of vicious outlaws he has helped send to the penitentiary has been released and is coming in on the noon train to take over the town, and, incidentally, to get the marshal.

What is the marshal's problem? Well, the prospect of having to face not just one but several very vicious, expert gunmen, bent on murder, is a situation calculated to bring a surge of genuine, honest fear to anyone save a complete moron. Genuine bravery is not simply the absence of fear. Otherwise, a clothing store dummy would be the bravest of us all. Bravery is, rather, the conquest of fear, for here again the line of reality and the law of reversal apply, and each emotion is coupled with its opposite. We humans can choose only which member of the couple we shall make prime and from which end of the line—cowardice or bravery—we shall operate.

But cowardice versus bravery is not our basic problem here, because the marshal has proved already that he is brave by once facing these killers and sending them to prison. What, then, is the emotion that keeps him in town to face them again?

We might name it *loyalty* and not be far wrong. After all, he is moved to be loyal to his duty and his town. But again we have special circumstances here: the marshal had already married, resigned, and planned to leave town before the outlaws arrive, remember. Loyalty can scarcely require him to continue to serve a town for which he no longer works.

But *honor* could make this demand. Especially since the marshal is a conscientious, honorable officer, taking his position and its duties and responsibilities seriously. Honor is one of the most powerful, creative emotions in this world.

Now we want to make it as difficult as possible for the marshal to make the "right" choice, because here is yet another paradox of plotting. To solve a plot problem, we always make it as difficult, as tough, as possible. If we can make it black enough at the climax, make it a spot calling for the supreme sacrifice, why virtually always we can resolve the story satisfactorily. As you will notice, this is a phenomenon not peculiar to fiction and plotting.

As the American Declaration of Independence put it: while evils are sufferable, mankind is more disposed to suffer; but when the evil becomes insufferable, then man acts. We apply this axiom literally in good plotting.

Make the problem worse and worse and worse! Make it as bad as you possibly can and then add some more! If you can get it black enough then inevitably, through reversal, you will arrive suddenly at unexpected *solution* and light. Which is another basic axiom so simple it is very hard to follow.

So–o, let's make our marshal's problem worse. Let's make his bride a pacifist, opposed to violence and killing. Let's make all the townspeople arrant cowards, afraid to face the deadly guns of the incoming killers, unwilling to take the first steps for their own protection. Let's have his promised help all run out on the marshal, so that as time for the noon train approaches he faces the prospect of going down to the station to face them absolutely alone, without, so it seems, one Chinaman's chance for survival.

But he doesn't have to stay and get killed. He's all ready

40

to leave with his bride. Let's make this decision extra dramatic: let's have him get in his buckboard with his grips and his bride and actually start to depart from this graceless, cowardly place whose men will dare nothing to aid their own defender.

[There was another man on another road once, pursuing a similarly wrong course. His name was Saul, and the road was the way to Damascus. What happened to him and how he became Paul, the greatest of all the apostles of Christ, is one of the most moving and dramatic of all religious stories.]

We know what our marshal will do. He will think of the women and children back there—helpless, innocent victims of their men folks' cowardice. He will think of what goes with being a peace officer—selfless devotion to duty, loyalty, courage, and, above all, honor. On his own dark road to Damascus our marshal will decide and act. For the sake of others, he will turn back.

Now what happens? The outlaws do not expect him. That's one advantage. With the advantage of surprise, courage, and being right, the marshal will get them, one by one. "No man in the wrong ever stood up to a man in the right who kept right on coming," said a dauntless old Texas Ranger, and it is as true today as it was in the Old West, as will be, please God, forever. At the climax of the gunplay we can have a most amazing thing happen to turn the tide.

The little bride, of course, will have told the marshal she wants no more of him, she is quitting him if he goes back, she will have no part of gunplay and violence. [We make it as tough as possible for the poor guy!] He faces his grim choice, so far as he knows, absolutely alone.

But the Lord is on his side. At the critical instant, when the marshal's back is turned, and from outside the window of the hotel one of the outlaws can get him, the little bride, standing inside, seizes a pistol and downs the outlaw, just in time. And the marshal triumphantly cleans up the last survivors of the gang and reclaims his bride.

It couldn't happen, logically. I am recounting the plot of the famous and very successful motion picture, *High Noon*, as you perhaps recognized. But it sold with tremendous éclat as fiction, and its like did happen, not once, but many times, and not alone in the West. History is filled with similar examples—the Spartans at Thermopylae, the Greeks at Salamis, the ragged Continentals at Valley Forge and Yorktown, the men of the Alamo in Texas. And sometimes they lived, sometimes they died, but what does that matter? They were sure they were right, as Davy Crockett said, and they went straight ahead.

In the brilliant San Antonio sunlight in front of the Alamo the tall men who died there for Texas liberty live forever in the cenotaph and statues, and in something more, something intangible. You can sense they are there. They died, yes. But they died right, on the way, and that also is the "happy ending."

This, then, is the essence of normal, forward plot, and always the more it seems to be different, the more, on closer inspection, you will find it to be the same old thing.

Pose a hard, emotional problem for your hero, remembering that the real battleground of story is inside his breast, and what he says and does outside is only the reflection of what is occurring inside. Make it the sort of problem that cannot be solved by intellect or ratiocination—there's a ten-dollar word of the sort one never uses in writing a good story! Add complications, making it worse and worse, harder and harder to make the "right" choice, until you have made it as black as you can, virtually impossible for your hero to make the right choice.

Remember, at the decision point he must make his choice

for the sake of others, or at least some other person. He must (1) decide, and (2) act upon this decision.

In reading published stories for technique it is sometimes difficult to spot the decision point. It is *not* an intellectual process, remember, and a clever writer will often cover it so smoothly that only by going back and rereading will you be able to find it. Sometimes decision and action will be combined, so that as the hero acts you know he must have decided and acted almost simultaneously.

In slick-paper magazine stories it is currently customary to add a realization section—usually several paragraphs, sometimes several pages—after the decision and action. This is where the hero realizes consciously what he has done and says as much, or sums it up. This is a second look, mind, and *not* the real decision and action, though it may often be mistaken for the climax.

Finally, in brief, let's look at the "minus," or "unhappy-ending" plot. It is the same as the "happy ending," except that at the decision point the hero gives way to the "wrong" emotion, makes the wrong choice, the wrong action, and so, by reversal in the denouement, ends up with nothing desirable, is miserable, regretful, and unhappy.

Suppose, for example, our marshal had elected to keep on running, had run clear off and abandoned the town to the mercies of the outlaws. We know very well what eventually would have happened to him.

He would have been miserably unhappy, despite the fact that he had saved his bride. Even though she was a pacifist, his wife would eventually have come to despise him as a coward. He would have found himself a man without honor and without friends. And at last, if he did not drink himself to death, as some did under similar circumstances, one of the vengeful outlaws, or perhaps a citizen of the town he had deserted, would have found and potted him anyway.

Having made the wrong choice, he would find, like the hero of a Greek tragedy, that he could not escape his fate.

Benedict Arnold, making the wrong choice, deciding to turn traitor, was showered with riches and honors by the British, but nevertheless was despised by them as well as hated by the Americans he had tried to betray. He died miserably unhappy. His is a typical "unhappy-ending" plot.

Now one final caution. The normal, forward plot I have here described is basically the Christian, religious thesis, which affirms that a man can be born again, that at the great decision point in his life, symbolically at least, he does die and then experience a rebirth in a new and finer form. The instant of transfiguration is a miracle, transcending human logic and logical expectation. It is what the Greek version of the New Testament calls δύναμις, "a work of power."

People who refuse to believe in miracles will not accept this Accordingly, in our modern, highly irreligious age, a great many so-called stories will be found, which, properly speaking, are not stories, or at least do not have plots, at all. Rather, they are character sketches, essays, parts of a plot in which the protagonist is brought up to the decision point and then simply stops there, or shies away from it, making no choice at all; there are backward stories—the "literary" form, self-nominated, which we shall examine presently— or diatribes against people who, for some reason, the writer and reader do not like.

For the literary plot there is, perhaps, some justification. As a complete reversal of the normal plot, it is, in effect, the back to a front, the completion of a great reality in this world. This, incidentally, is the type of plot the classic Greeks portrayed in their tragedies—man trapped by his destiny, unable to escape. It is also the sort of story high school teen-agers, fumbling to come up with their first plots, first stories, almost invariably produce. For this bleak futility Christianity supplies the answer.

44

But for these other alleged "stories," and for the curious people who read them, people who cannot tell a stone from bread, there is not much to be said. There is, so far as I know, no cure for lack of brains or absence of taste.

Consider now the time of the normal, forward story, either "plus" or "minus," and you have, I hope, a fair preliminary picture.

The time of the normal, forward story is "now," no matter in what age it is set. And the direction of view, the progression, is from "now" toward the future.

This also is religious, you will notice, since looking back is specifically listed as an evil in the Bible (Lot's wife), while heaven is depicted as a timeless place of no night, presumably an eternal, joyous "now." But notice something more before we finish this chapter. In the normal, forward story each sentence must be written as though it were happening "right now," and each next paragraph must seem to hang in the future, no matter how many times the reader reads and rereads the story!

Note also that the decision-and-action affects the future, not the past. What the hero does at the decision point changes the course of his whole future life. And, more, he is free to act at this point, free to choose between this and that, a liberty not available in the literary story.

Looking back through time, as a literary story does, obviously a decision means nothing practical, since it is impossible to change the past. True, I may like or dislike some past event. But that means little. I cannot change it now. Nor, looking backward, do I have any real use for a moral sense of direction, since I cannot use it backward to escape or reach any past incident. Accordingly, as we shall see, the so-called literary story tends, at least, to be both amoral and without sense of direction—which, as used here, tend, of course, to be the same thing.

Commercially, the forward, normal story is by far the

most popular and profitable, with the genuine happy ending, of course, much preferred to the unhappy ending. Do not let the learned ones misguide you on this.

Any fool can make mistakes and end unhappily. There is something, perhaps, to be gained from his example. But for most people it is precious little. But to do exactly the right thing, at the right time, under the right circumstances, to reach the happy ending—that, now, is precious hard, in fiction or in fact! Which is precisely why, in fiction, it is so much preferred, so much more the mark of a master writer, and so enormously more profitable to learn to do.

CHAPTER IV

The Literary Plot

YOU WILL NEED TO GRASP the different ways it is possible to look at time in order to make sense of this chapter. There are three ways. The first, which is almost never attempted in fiction, and never successfully in my opinion, is the actually timeless aspect of heaven—or hell. Anyone who has endured a long sick spell, or some injury which seemed to take forever to improve, will know what I mean here. And I have a friend who was once trapped in a coal mine cave-in. In the strained, never-ending waiting in the black void, waiting for perhaps rescue, perhaps death, he learned, so he said, about that timeless eternity that underlies all earthly time—time that can be, to repeat, either heaven's immortal bliss or the everlasting torment of hell.

This sort of timing we simply do not know how to convey to readers who have never endured or enjoyed it. So we leave this to the priests and ministers, the teachers of religion. But there remain two other ways which we can and do use—and now be patient with me, because in all probability you know one of these very well but have never realized, or perhaps cannot grasp, the other, at least not without all sorts of patience and effort.

Here is another plotting detail like those hidden faces in the puzzle picture. Getting angry, trying to force matters, will get you nowhere. Instead, you must sit and look patiently, trying to clear your mind, trying to free yourself from all those imprisoning habitual concepts, until at long, long last the faces suddenly emerge, the picture comes to you.

Just as the story of Lot's wife in the Bible tries to tell us, there is a paralyzing, objective way of seeing reality in this world. And there is also an opposite, subjective, religious way. Nor is the Bible the only place that tells us this. Even the ancients recognized this duality, because the Greeks also had a name for it, and a legend—that of the Medusa.

In the biblical story of Lot's wife, you will remember, Lot, a righteous man, was warned by the Lord to remove himself and his family from the incredibly wicked city of Sodom, because the city was slated for destruction. He and his were also cautioned not to look back as they fled. But Lot's wife, with feminine curiosity, disobeyed the injunction and did glance back at the awful destruction behind. Thereupon she was turned into a pillar of salt.

Let me say again, in these stories seek the content and not merely the surface. The story about Mary giving Johnny two apples, Johnny already has one apple, now how many does he have—this in your elementary arithmetic was not intended as an entertaining story about Mary and Johnny. Neither are these stories which have come down to us through the ages intended merely to amuse, or to be taken at face value only. You must bear in mind always that the writers, or tellers of the stories, had to use the language and concepts of their times; they had to communicate. With our far more elaborate and technical vocabulary, we would say it very differently. But this difference in language and illustration does not change the basic truths at all.

The Greek legend is even more explicit. The Medusa was one of the Gorgon sisters, terrifying furies whose very look turned all observers to stone. But the hero, Perseus, disposed of the ugly menace quite neatly by reversal. He did not look at the snake-haired destroyer. Instead, he polished a shield until it was mirror bright, looked only at the reflection in that, and, thus guided, lopped off the Medusa's head.

48

Now let's see what these and similar stories mean in plain, modern English.

In the medieval centuries, the ages of belief, man looked from the present toward the future. He concerned himself not at all with science, technology, medicine, astronomy, all the million and one objective fields which we consider so all-important. He did not even set down much history! Instead, he looked toward heaven and saw this world as a strange place of trials and testing, a sort of waiting room for the saved and the damned of eternity. We call these the Dark Ages, though with a few more atomic bombs and other objective flashes of enlightenment we may change our minds.

When the Renaissance and Reformation came along, human beings actually saw their world turned over. It was literally a revolution—a reversal—and a most tremendous one.

Medieval man had started his picture of this world, or of all reality, from his first personal subjective self. Or, to be more precise about it, since he couldn't see himself— your own face is the one you will never meet, never see direct, in this world, isn't it?—medieval man started accordingly from the nearest thing he could see, the book.

If you will consult your oculist, he will tell you there are two points of clearest vision in your range of sight—a near point, so-called, a *punctum proximum,* and a distance point, a *punctum remotum*. Curiously, you have both these points for almost anything you look at.

Diamond-point type, for example, can be seen by the normal eye most clearly at six inches and again at twenty inches. For other type or objects similar intervals apply, the distances varying, of course, with the size of the object. But the nearest we can see anything very clearly is six or seven inches; the most distant—well, the most distant objects we have to practice on are the stars.

49

Now you will notice that as man began to try to understand himself and his problems he concentrated on these two points. Either, as did the astrologers, he tried to read his destiny in the stars; or, trying to learn from the other end of the line, he sought to read omens in the entrails of animals, in the lines of human hands, the shape of heads, the wrinkles of people's faces, and the like.

He was half-right, half-wrong in each of these extreme choices, because he had not yet realized—for that matter, have we?—that reality is a line with two ends, both of which matter. We can, we must, choose one as our landmark, our prime beginning point. But that does not eliminate the other or even forbid us to use it. Let's see now the difference between medieval and Reformation-Renaissance modern man.

To medieval man the landmark, the beginning place, the near point was par excellence the book, held inches from his nose. At first this book was the Bible. Then, as the survey extended into areas not specifically covered by the book, other books were accepted also—Galen, for example, in medicine and Aristotle in science.

But to go behind these books, to question and disturb the prime landmark, the beginning point, was taboo! It would, quite understandably, upset the whole existing scheme of things, lay the mighty low, impoverish the rich, make beggars kings. Can't have that sort of thing, you realize, harrumph, egad! So—as one quaint result—for thirteen hundred years nobody ever officially counted his own ribs, nobody ever examined his own big toe—the first thing a baby might do!

But the human body was behind the book, as you can see, in taboo territory. The great book, the Bible, said that God took one of Adam's ribs to make Eve. Nothing was said about the Lord's thoughtfully replacing the rib, as you know He'd do. So, for thirteen centuries men believed that men had one less rib than women: and for nearly as long, since this was from Galen, they believed also that there was a special bone in the big toe, a resurrection bone, by which one would be lifted up on resurrection morning.

When Vesalius finally came along, in the irreverent new dawn of the objective view, and exposed these, plus a couple of hundred other errors, in his magnificent *Anatomy*, he was very nearly burned at the stake for his trouble! So easy is it to make humanity see something new!

Copernicus, most cautiously; Galileo, more bravely, though he also quailed and recanted when faced with the terror; and Bruno, rashest of all, since he was burned at the stake for his pains—these pioneers in effect simply denied the primacy of the book as the landmark, the beginning point, and returned instead to the opposite landmark used by the ancients, the Babylonians and Chaldeans, that is, to the distant stars. They chose the nearest one, perhaps for caution's sake. But our sun is a star, for all that, and it is a distance point.

And if we are going to base all our mapping, our concept of reality, on that, how different it will be from the picture based on the book!

Do not misread me here! As Galileo himself said, it is as possible for a scientist as for a priest to reach God, and that I also devoutly believe. In the end, whether the territory be surveyed from the near point or distance point, no matter which is set as prime, if the surveying be correctly done, the maps will be the same. It is only in the making, and unfinished appearances, that they are diametrically opposite.

The good surveyor, of course, uses both near and distance points, both landmark and opposite end of the base line, to make his map complete and accurate. He is not such an idiot as to consider the rodman out there as his enemy, or even as his intellectual inferior. Nor does the rodman believe he could do better without the surveyor.

Yet just such stupidities do we find in the literary world, when pundits discuss stories and plot. Let's hope here that you and I are not quite this idiotic.

Now the *literary plot:*

We saw that the normal, forward plot began with an emotional problem faced "now" by the hero. The action moves from the present into the future, with little or no looking back to the past. When a backward look is taken, incidentally, it is either retrospection—which is thoroughly disliked by editors unless it is so competently written that the reader understands it is about the hero, thinking right now, and only secondarily about the past events of which he is thinking—or, if the VP character lapses completely into memories, it is called flashback. And, once again, the proper way to write it is in the "happening-now" timing. A device called a *transition* is used to get into, and emerge from, flashback, and this we shall examine in a later chapter. But the literary plot, with a wholly different timing, was a far different version of all of these things.

The literary plot looks back through time, not forward. It tries, at least, to eliminate personal viewpoint. Like a statistical table, it is not concerned with the individual, or any singular person, but instead only with the objective plural, with the pluralistic view.

Actually, of course, there is no such thing as an objective view. No human has ever stood on the sun and looked at the earth, to see how we appear from the opposite end of the line. Nobody has ever merged with a mirror, to know definitely how much of what we see reflected is actually in and from the mirror and how much we simply add on the subjective end of the line.

But we can imagine ourselves doing these things. Like

a small boy playing cowboy, our concept is doubtless a far, far cry from the real thing. Yet if it satisfies us, perhaps it serves.

There is a special kind of viewpoint ordinarily used in literary story writing, which is also opposite to normal viewpoint. It is called *resection* and is similar to the surveying method a ship's navigator or a land surveyor uses when he wants to locate himself.

For example, a ship is coming into a harbor. The navigator can see a lighthouse far over to one side and a promontory peak off to the other side somewhere. He has a map of the harbor on which these points are located.

Now by taking bearings on the two points and drawing properly located lines on his chart back from the points, he can locate himself. He will be "at" the spot where the lines intersect. Obviously, the two points must not be on opposite ends of the same diameter, which we will discover has an artistic as well as mathematical significance. But more about that later. Our navigator here has just turned a trick in resection. It is a tricky trick, so let's look closely at what he did.

He triangulated in reverse for one thing. He knew the map location of the lighthouse and of the peak. But he did not know his own. He used the line between lighthouse and peak as the base of his triangle, and by erecting the sides with the proper compass bearings, he established the apex of the triangle, the spot where he was "at."

Now normally, if he had just been looking at the lighthouse, the base of the triangle would have been the space between his two eyes, and the lighthouse would have been "at" where the lines of sight crossed. Notice this is just the opposite of what the navigator did to locate himself.

But now notice also in both cases he actually operated from where he physically, bodily, was "at" and *not* from the end of the line where he was not. He couldn't operate from where he wasn't. That's so elementary it sounds silly; nevertheless, it is not understood by many literate persons.

In *resectional viewpoint* in fiction we do precisely the same thing. Our VP character is a sort of little lost soul in the middle of chaos. The line-of-view work begins at various points around him. Eventually—as much to our surprise as his—the lines intersect, and we discover our hero is somewhere there in the middle. Let's make up a fair example here to illustrate what I mean:

> The room crouched—evil, waiting. A decaying odor oozed up from the ragged, stained carpet as though it hated all the things that bruised it. The windows stared inward through sightless, blurred, evil eyes. Dust lay thick on the sills, on the arms of the sagging sofa, and even in the panels of the closed door which the little man kept watching. Half-sunk into the ruinous cushions of the sofa, he kept squirming, sniffing at the dust in the air, glancing from door to windows to chair and always back again to the door.

In this, as you see, we do not even know anyone is in the room for several sentences. We do get subjective impressions of parts of the room—the fetid odor, the carpet, the soiled windows, the door, etc. Eventually we discover that a little man is in the center of all this doing the observing. He is actually the focus of the view, but in place of starting from him and working outward, we begin from the perimeter and work in.

This is certainly not omniscient viewpoint. The view of the Lord is not from soiled windows and dirty carpet. This is merely a simple reversal of human viewpoint. But sometime we have to get to the VP character in the middle. When we discover him, we know what is happening.

It is typical of literary viewpoint that it tries to deal with the VP character as objectively as possible, calling him "the little man" as though he were a complete stranger, trying hard to make him an object rather than subject. Reader identification with the VP character is avoided as much as possible. The general idea seems to be to make the reader reject rather than accept the character. Which is understandable enough when one realizes that this is back-handed fiction, doing the whole thing in reverse.

All sorts of combinations of resectional and intersectional viewpoint will be found in so-called "literary" stories. But a masterly example of how to handle this technique can be studied in Luigi Pirandello's *The House of Agony*.

Now the order of the literary plot:

In reverse of the normal plot, the literary plot begins with the *answer*. From this it moves backward to the action and decision. There can be no real free decision in past time, naturally. You can't unwin the battle of Waterloo or not sink the Titanic. So, no matter what the hero tries to decide, tries to do, either course leads him to the same place—to the *question* or *problem*, where the normal story begins.

With such a peculiar backward way of looking at things, of accepting as real only things in past time, you can see why the literary story tends to be amoral. Moral direction is something we need to go from the present into the future. Deceiving ourselves into believing that we can move from the present into the past or even from the past into the present, we still have no need for moral compasses or directions. They can serve no useful purposes. The story is as fixed and frozen as a Siberian tundra, and the hero as imbedded in it as a woolly mammoth.

Please understand I am not saying the literary story is not a legitimate art form. It bears about the same relationship to the normal story that still-life paintings or abstractions do to action pictures or portraits. It is certainly not superior to the normal plot, no matter what teachers of English may have told you. But it is not to be despised.

A masterful example of the literary plot can be found in Guy de Maupassant's "The Jewels."[1]

This, you will remember, is a story about a little government clerk who has a beautiful and talented wife. Her one weakness is for costume jewelry. But since she spends apparently nothing for the stuff, since she is otherwise so wonderful a housekeeper and manager, he indulges her in this one foible. He is perfectly happy.

Now, this is the "they-lived-happily-afterwards" ending, the answer to the normal plot. But here it comes at the beginning of the story.

Then the wife dies. To his amazement and dismay the little clerk finds that he cannot live alone on the salary the wife stretched to include even luxuries for two. At last he is forced to take a bucketful or so of the costume jewelry down to the jeweler's to see if it has any value at all, if he can sell it. He discovers it is not phony. Instead, it is real— real gold, real jewels, and very valuable!

So here is our hero up against his realization, which normally comes after the *decision* in the plot. There can be only one way the wife could have gotten all this expensive trumpery. She had been unfaithful to him. She had a lover. And he, the little clerk, is a cuckold.

Now comes the attempted decision and action. Shall the clerk sell the jewelry, the fruits of his shame, and take the money? Or shall he throw the stuff in the gutter and stalk off, outraged?

Actually, it makes no difference which course he chooses. Neither will change the past. He will remain a betrayed husband, a despicable cuckold, no matter what he does now. But being a thrifty Frenchman, he chooses to sell the jewelry and take the money.

It is enough to permit him to retire. Presently he finds

[1] In American translations this story is usually titled, "The False Gems."

himself another wife who is undoubtedly virtuous. But she makes him supremely miserable.

Observe now what we've got: a plot that begins with the reward or answer, moves thence to realization, then to the meaningless decision and action, and ends at last at the problem—just where a normal story would begin.

Suppose now we flip this into a normal, forward plot to make the difference as clear by contrast as possible. We shall use the wife, not the husband, as the principal character and tell the story from "now" forward in time.

The wife has had a lover who has given her a great amount of expensive jewelry. She has told her husband it is just costume junk and has deceived him completely. The lover is dead now, and the wife is certain she has gotten away with her deceit.

This part we will tell in flashback in the wife's thoughts as the story proceeds. As the story opens, the phone is ringing. The wife answers and it is a doctor calling from the hospital. Hubby has been in a very serious accident and is all mashed to bits.

It will take a small fortune to get him repaired and out of the hospital, the wife soon discovers. He has no insurance and she has no money—nothing except her jewelry. So now she is up against her great problem.

Shall she sell the jewelry and pay to have hubby renovated? In which case eventually he will have to be told where the money came from. Or shall she keep her jewelry and her secret and let her husband suffer, perhaps die?

You should take note here that this decision will affect the future, not the past. The question is what the husband will do when he finds out where she got the money. The wife is only too unhappily certain she can guess what he will do. He'll just kill her. But if she doesn't spend the money on him, he will be a cripple or he will die.

This being a normal, "happy-ending" plot, with a

"right" and "wrong" direction to the decision, you know very well what she'll do. She elects to sell the jewelry and get hubby out of hock. Of course, when he is recovering nicely, she has to tell him how she got the money.

Now comes our twist, or reversal. The husband is not in the least enraged. On the contrary, he says this proves his wife must love him to make such a sacrifice. He adores her and all is forgiven. And besides—

Let's add a continental touch for a tag. And besides, he knew all along what she was doing. He was getting a small commission from the jeweler for each piece of jewelry the lover bought.

I think this ought to do the literary plot!

CHAPTER V

The Universal Plot Patterns

WHEREVER YOU GO in this world, to whatever continent, island, nation, or race, always if you will closely examine the stories told there you will find that they are built on the same framework, the same basic pattern. They are really the same story, no matter how great the seeming differences because of different building materials. And this, on first recognition, is amazing.

But then, on second thought, it is not surprising at all. On the contrary, why should it not be so? Everywhere all men, of all races and climes, look out at their world and its problems through identically the same sort of eyes. In all places the basic problem is the same. And this has been true, so far as we know, through all recorded history, since the first man climbed down from his tree and became something different, a human being, a man.

Yet again, it is incredible that so many billions, over so many thousands of years, could have seen *what* they saw, could have sensed as they did that there was something identical in all these seeming infinite differences, that some quality made one of all humanity and all humanity's troubled ones. Yet no one saw *how*. This is not quite fair, of course. The mystics did see, yet could not communicate their vision; and the great religious figures, the founders, both saw and communicated, albeit in a style wholly incomprehensible to most moderns. In our language, what was it they saw?

They saw what I have here called reversal. It is the essence of mysticism. It is the heart secret of religion and,

59

above all, of the great Judeo-Christian tradition of which we are a part. It is metaphysical and supernatural. And yet it is also objective and physical; it is wholly real. In its practical aspects, at least, it can be understood and applied by anyone of even moderate intelligence, and it can be taught by anyone with understanding and good will.

I know this is so bcause I have seen it done.

The problem is that man is an overlay animal. Evolving through the long stages of creation (for true creation is a continuing process, a wave in motion, an applied genius, remember, and only secondarily an accomplished fact), man has acquired two natures, two kinds of intelligence.

This is not in the least mystical, no matter what the weird psychologists and psychiatrists and their ilk may have made of it. Their "unconscious," or "subconscious," mind is nothing in the world but the old amoeba creature that man was before he became man, before he was given eyes to see. Their "ego," or "conscious" mind, is merely the overlaying intelligence that has come with the acquisition of eyes with which to see. You have only to notice what consciousness means—*the awareness of relationships with external objects*—to begin, at least, to set yourself aright.

The original living creature in this world undoubtedly was just like the still-with-us amoeba, the tiny, one-celled being that swims by the billions in every pool of stagnant water.

What the amoeba learns, what it can and does learn, it finds out by direct contact.

It has no organs for handling intelligence from a distance. Instead, it must touch that which it knows, must grasp or reject it; and accordingly we know that it must and does have the fundamentals of at least two emotions, two "feelings"—attraction and revulsion, love and hate. We humans ourselves have no greater basis for our emotions. These are the founding two, and all others are merely conditioned yeses or noes. We can know also what we mean when we say that we have a real grasp of a subject. We mean we have taught it to the amoeba-man inside, who thinks only in feelings, who knows nothing else save gradations of yes and no.

But with evolution came more complicated creatures and eventually the supreme organ for reporting events and conditions at a distance, the eye.

Now examine the eyes of living creatures, and you will discover a bewildering multiplicity of forms. For one instantly interesting detail, you will find that the eyes of many insects, of ants and bees for immediate examples, are compound. That is, the creature sees not one image but instead literally hundreds of images of whatever it may chance to look at; and accordingly its world must be like that of the complete scientist—objectively plural on both ends.

But look still closer and you see that all these seemingly altogether different eyes have one feature in common. *All of them invert the image. All turn the picture upside down.*

The human cortex, the human overbrain, developed to handle the tidings from the eyes which are a direct part of it, reports that the vase, the lamp, or whatever, is upside down, hanging like a mirage in air. The human hands, the eyes of that inner amoeba-man, reach out to grasp the object and flatly contradict the eyes. And always, always, always, without a single exception, whenever man really masters any problem, really grasps and solves any difficulty, he does so by resolving this dispute, by learning to turn the problem over so that it may be grasped and handled by that inner amoeba-man.

The intellect alone solves nothing whatever and never has in all history. Which is the hardest of all paradoxes to grasp.

Nevertheless, this is the reason the great church fathers have always distrusted the intellect and the reports of the senses; and it is the reason why in the religion or the mythology of nearly all peoples you find some variation of the reversal story, the parable which endeavors to state this universal truth.

To the ancient Egyptians, the story was the legend of Osiris, murdered by Set, the principle of evil, resurrected by Isis, his wife, and avenged by Horus, his son. It was the fish gods, coming from the depths of the sea to instruct men in arts and letters, to the Chaldeans. To the Persians and later Romans it was the Mithraic legends. For the Greeks it was the tale of Persephone or Proserpina, kidnapped by Pluto, lord of the underworld, rescued (for six months of each year) by Mercury. It was the Eleusinian mysteries of the ancient world. And the Christian Bible is full of similar stories, disclosing, as a great pope said, a truth while at the same time they cloak a mystery.

The Garden of Eden story in Genesis is such an account. Man in the Garden, moved by his feelings, is amoeba-man. Man outside, "his eyes opened," possessed of exterior, visual knowledge, is the objective, visual man. The account of the flood, known also to the Chaldeans and Babylonians, in chapter 22 of Genesis, recounting the willingness of Abraham to sacrifice Isaac, his son, for the sake of the Lord, and its tremendous reversal in the New Testament; the Life of Christ, God sacrificing his Son for the sake of sinful Man—these are more.

Forgive me if I repeat. The inner amoeba-man can be taught nothing except by direct contact, by actual doing, by endless repetition. Rhythms and rhythmic responses must be built in so that they are deeper than thought, so that they are, as nearly as we can make them, automatic. Only when this has happened can we say truly that we have grasped and mastered any subject; only when the transition is made do we have the real answer to any problem. It is, I am saying, exactly like when you learned to swim, or ride a bicycle, or touch type. Once gained, such knowledge never deserts you.

Now here again, before we look at examples from all over the world, is the *basic pattern of plot* and its three incarnations:

Two emotions—*love* versus *honor*, *ambition* versus *fear*, *greed* versus *loyalty*, or whatever—contend in the same living breast. The story is a moving process, an action, a journey; and as with any real motion, it is oriented. One side, one emotion, is "right," and the other is left or "wrong." But as the story progresses, we are increasingly uncertain which is which. And at the climax, the decision point, about three-fourths of the way through the plot, we cannot see our way at all, because we have arrived at the black moment, the focal point of reversal, the place where visual, objective reason fails, the instant of death and rebirth, the place of transition through the narrow gate from the world of outer, objective, visual man to the inner world of amoeba-man. And I say this not disparagingly. This is the reversal with which we deal: to get back to God we must return to the source of life, the Creator; and God began his creation of life in this earth with the single, one-celled creature. This path we have within ourselves, from the instant of conception until we have evolved into what we are today.

At the instant of decision the hero goes through the surface of the mirror, through the glass into that other world. Very definitely we can know some few things about this dark passage. From the literature of all nations, from the recorded experience of millions of men and women, from the patient workers in the laboratories of science (for God is to be found there too, just as Galileo said, though sometimes it is a bit difficult to detect Him there), and from the whole experience of mankind, we can know these details:

The significant phenomenon is reversal. In an instant, just as though we actually walked right through a vanishing point, right through the reflecting surface of a mirror, up becomes down, left changes to right, and right to left. One second we are going, the next coming. But in this transformation one factor remains constant. That is the guiding, right line.

    ·   If we can determine which is "right," and go straight through on this line, hanging to it by blind faith, then on the other side we shall find ourselves still in the "right," even though there we may be coming, where here we are going. This is what the hero does in a normal, "happy-ending" story.

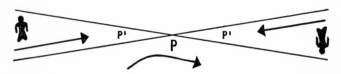

The accompanying diagram, perhaps, will make this clearer than any possible words. Imagine it as a road up which you are traveling, guiding right, as shown by the arrow, A. You arrive at Point P' and there, just ahead, is the vanishing point, enclosed in the black moment, a dark fog through which you cannot see. How, now, do you proceed?

Well, there are two things you can choose between. You can try to be logical and cling to the right-hand curb. In which case you will "go crooked" at Point P. in the middle of the darkness, and emerge precisely where you do not want to be, on the wrong side of the road, heading the wrong way. This is the "unhappy-ending" type plot.

Or you can, like Davy Crockett, be sure you're right and go straight ahead. In which case you will emerge on the right side of the road, the "happy ending."

The correction which you make or fail to make just before taking the crucial step is essentially that you'd use to spear a fish, a foot or two down in clear water. Because of refraction, the fact that light bends when passing from one medium to another of different density, you will see the fish apparently to one side and considerably higher than his actual position. But this positive report of your senses you will discard, "sacrifice," because experience or instruction has taught you about refraction. You will strike not at the fish where you see him but instead at another specific spot you have learned to locate intuitively, the exact place where he seems not to be. A second later, if your orientation work has been correct, you have the tangible reason for your great "sacrifice," in the form of the successfully speared fish. You have also demonstrated why the end cannot be argued as justification for the course, the means. Instead, the means, *the direction taken,* must justify itself.

Going straight on the right course, when our hero arrives on the other side, he finds that right has remained right. But the other emotion, the other side of the road, has swung clear over and we now have its inversion. Since all emotions are coupled with their opposites, inverted hate, for instance, becomes love; or greed, unselfishness—a very famous example of this last inversion is found in Charles Dickens' immortal *Christmas Carol,* in which miserly Scrooge makes just such a reversal.

Finally, with one emotion, the "right" one, remaining constant, and one inverting and reversing itself, we no longer have a conflict, and the plot-problem is solved. Now both emotions are compatible, on the same side, united in a satisfying unit answer.

As a footnote, take one more look at the diagram. Notice that refraction occurs only when we are looking at the fish from an oblique angle. If we were directly above him, with the light overhead, so that it went straight down and came right back to our eye, we could strike right where we see him and spear our fish. This ability to see directly is probably that possessed by the saints and the true clairvoyants. All of us experience brief instants of it sometime in our lives. And it is what makes us "sacrifice" that seemingly real, yet actually crooked, line in favor of that straight, "right" line which shows nothing at its end and appears to promise us nothing.

I hope the theologians will not quarrel with me when I say that to me, in my simplicity, God is as real in that which He creates as in the tremendous, intangible principles whereby He created all things. I do not believe we can ever wholly understand these principles, and accordingly most theological speculation is barren and vain. But I think also we may hope to see through the things to the principles that make and operate them. This much I think God expects of us.

I cannot believe He would give me eyes and not expect me to use them, or give me a mind which I was not supposed to employ.

As a complete reversal of the whole forward pattern of story-plot, we have also, as we have noticed, the so-called "literary" plot, in which the whole business is seen in the past, is looked at backwards, and accordingly is frozen into stone. There are, then, three basic types, three variations of the one universal plot. We can name them "Type A, happy ending"; "Type B, unhappy ending"; and "Type C," the literary plot, in which, no matter whether we start from the happy or the unhappy fork, proceeding backwards we arrive inevitably at the question, where we stop to wail.

Now let's look at the promised examples from all over the world:

Type A, happy ending: "A Chaparral Christmas Gift," by O. Henry. *American.*

I-nitial character. By this I mean the character the story is actually about. He may or may not be the VP character. Just as with vanishing points and perspectives in painting, so also in writing there are a number of possible variations in VP. In this story the VP character is actually the author, O. Henry, partially disguised as a second person. The tale was written at a time when American VP work was in a transitional stage—from the very simple, primitive form in which the reader or listener supplied virtually all the subjective end, toward the present stage in which a great deal of the subjective orientation is provided for on the page.

The I-nitial character in this is Johnny McRoy, the Frio Kid.

Problem: Love versus *hate.*

Rosita McMullen is beloved by both Madison Lane, a young rancher, and Johnny McRoy, a cowboy. She chooses Lane. In a fit of jealous hate and rage Johnny invades the wedding, tries to shoot Madison and Rosita, and does kill a guest before he is driven off. Thereafter Johnny becomes a vicious outlaw and killer, the Frio Kid.

Some years later the Lanes give a Christmas party at their ranch. The Frio Kid hears of it and decides to ride over and finish the business by killing the man he has hated for so long. Rosita has feared just such a visit, and Lane sets his cowboys on guard.

But nothing suspicious happens. Santa Claus arrives and distributes presents. A guest asks casually if Rosita is still afraid of the Frio Kid, and she says she has almost gotten over that and adds that she believes he has a spot of good in him. As she turns away she bumps into Santa Claus, who remarks that he overheard her, just as he was reaching into his pocket for a present for her husband. But now he's decided to give her a present instead. She'll find it in the next room.

Rosita goes in and only Madison, her husband, is there. Santa hasn't left any present, Madison says, unless he, Madison is the gift. The next day the news comes that the Frio Kid has been killed in the night by a sheepherder, and, curiously, the Kid was dressed in a Santa Claus disguise.

Comment: The story is the Frio Kid's. The plot-problem, as stated, is *love* (for Rosita) versus *hate* (for Lane) —both of which emotions are in the Kid's breast. The decision point is where the disguised Kid, hearing Rosita defend him, decides not to follow the dictates of hate and kill Lane but instead to let love be his guide. So, because he loves Rosita, he presents her Madison's life as a Christmas present. Curiously, although in the end the Kid is killed, this is a happy ending.

The Kid has gone out on the right road at the last, the right way. Which is what matters. We are concerned in this story not with things and their objective aspects but instead with the great intangibles, of which the very greatest, to us, is right direction. The question of whether the hero lives or dies at the end of the tale is not material, although ordinarily, of course, we let him live. But, living or dead, he must pass out of the story "going right," to make a happy ending.

Type B, unhappy ending: "The Piece of String," by Guy de Maupassant. *French.*

I-nitial character: Maître Hauchecorne.

Problem: Miserliness versus *honor.*

Maître Hauchecorne, miserly yet honorable Norman peasant, spies a piece of string on the road. He is an old-string saver, yet he knows people will despise him as a miser if he is seen picking up string. Regardless, he decides (the "wrong" course) to pick it up.

Very speedily he discovers this was indeed a wrong decision. He realizes, too late, that he is being observed in the very act. Shamed, he compounds his error by hiding the string and pretending it was something else. He is accused later of having found and kept a lost pocketbook.

He protests his innocence and honor loudly and angrily, but no one believes him. Even after the pocketbook is found, malicious jokers still pretend to disbelieve his story. So, heartbroken, Maître Hauchecorne dies, still protesting vainly that he was an honest man and that it was just a piece of string.

Type C, backward plot: "A Little Cloud," by James Joyce. *Irish.*

I-nitial character: Little Chandler.

Problem: Envy versus *domestic bliss.*

Little Chandler, commonplace clerk, has a brief reunion with an old school chum, Ignatius Gallaher, now a successful, dashing newspaperman. Returning home, Little Chandler realizes that he is bitterly envious. He regards his colorless wife and dingy flat and thinks vaguely that maybe he, too, could write a book, make a fortune from it, and escape.

But he can't. Even when he tries to read Byron's poems, the howling of the baby makes it impossible. It is all very futile and so, so-o-o-o sad.

Comment: Note that the story begins not with a problem, but instead with a joyful reunion, the sort of thing one would expect at the end. It proceeds next to a vague regret for decisions and actions past (marrying instead of becoming a writer) and then to a vain effort to decide and do something about it. But since the way of life, the wife, the baby, etc., all are the results of past actions none of which can be undone now, there is nothing Little Chandler can do except weep, and at the end of the story face his problem—backwards!

Type A, happy ending: "The Sire de Maletroit's Door," by Robert Louis Stevenson. *English.*

I-nitial character: Denis de Beaulieu.

Problem: Pride versus *love.*

In this very famous story is a masterly plot, an ingenious presentation of the posed problem in three versions. Discovering that his beloved niece, Blanche, is engaged in a surreptitious love affair with an unknown gallant, possibly besmirching the family pride, a stiff-backed old French aristocrat, the Sire de Maletroit, sets a trap for her young man. Into it falls Denis de Beaulieu, proud young cavalier and soldier. He is not the man. But De Maletroit introduces the captured Denis to Blanche as her lover and despite the young couple's frantic protests that they have never even seen each other before says cheerily he thinks otherwise. Eh, but no matter! He, De Maletroit, has tried to catch Blanche's lover for her. The family honor is involved. So now Blanche weds Denis, or Uncle de Maletroit just hangs the young man. He gives the youngsters two hours to make up their minds.

There you have it: *pride* versus *love* in three aspects. Uncle, Blanche, and Denis—each has his or her own version, own style of the problem. But Denis is the VP character, the Abraham of this tale, so it is principally his first version that we follow.

What does Denis decide and do? You know. Regardless of whether you ever heard this tale before or not, you know intuitively. Swallowing his foolish young pride that would lead him to a senseless death and make a beautiful young girl unhappy to have been the cause of it, *for the sake of love*, Denis asks Blanche to marry him. Blanche makes a similar happy sacrifice and consents. And proud old Uncle lovingly welcomes a new nephew.

Type B, unhappy ending: "The Work of Art," by Anton Chekhov. *Russian.*

I-nitial character: Doctor Koshelkov.

Problem: Priggishness versus *gratitude.*

A grateful patient presents Doctor Koshelkov with a rather daring work of art, a bronze candelabrum, supported by two female nudes. The priggish doctor ungratefully gives it away ("wrong" decision). The recipient is similarly priggish and passes it on. The eventual result, of course, is the delighted return of the original patient with the news that he has just found and bought an exact mate for the doctor's candelabrum, and now the medico can have a pair.

Comment: The viewpoint work in this story is so typically Russian that it deserves notice. Actually, the work of art itself, the candelabrum, is the VP. It is the only point in the tale from which all of the story can be seen and heard, as the story is told by Chekhov. The Russian inability to tell subjects from objects, or separate their rights from their leftists, displays itself not only in their government; it is inherent also in their art.

Type C, backward plot: "The House of Agony," by Luigi Pirandello. *Italian.*

I-nitial character: The anonymous caller.

Problem: Stoicism versus *compassion.*

This is a classic example of resectional viewpoint and as such is worth studying. The never-named "caller" we discover sitting in a fifth-floor apartment room, waiting for his host. He has no real problem as the story opens, and we do not even know he is there until the author has spent considerable wordage closing in on him from several sides, describing the surrounding furniture and room. But eventually we realize the VP is "somebody," in the center, and that he is idly watching the open window, where a cat is trying to catch a swallow. The cat is about to tip over a large, window-ledge geranium pot, probably to send it crashing down right on the head of some luckless passer-by on the sidewalk five stories below.

Now if "the caller" drives the cat or the swallows away, they will return. If he moves the pot, the stupid servant will replace it. He can at best only postpone the tragedy; he cannot avert it. He watches the cat jostle the pot until he can stand it no longer. Then (vain attempt at decision and action) he flees. And, of course, he arrives on the sidewalk below just in time to get hit by the pot—very fatally, we trust.

Why the jerk couldn't have thrust his head out the window, yelled "Look out below!" and heaved the pot, or cat, or both, the author does not say. But, of course, this would have been crude interference with literary futility and implacable destiny.

Type B, unhappy ending: "The Lagoon," by Joseph Conrad. *Polish.*

I-nitial character: Arsat, the Malay.

Problem: Sexual love versus *fraternal love.*

Here is another variation in VP work. The viewpoint is a character simply called "the white man," but the story is that of a principal character at whom the white man looks, Arsat the Malay. This is *bystander viewpoint,* in other words.

Arsat, the Malay, has enlisted his brother to help him elope with one of the Rajah's women. They are pursued. The brother drops back to delay the pursuers, while Arsat gets the woman into the boat. Suddenly Arsat hears his brother call for help and (the decision and action) elects to escape with the girl, rather than go back to help his brother. The brother is killed. Now (the "minus" answer) the woman is dying of some mysterious ailment, and Arsat is desolate.

Type B, unhappy ending: "The Louse and the Butterfly." *Trobriand Islands folk tale.*

I-nitial character: The louse.

Problem: Ambition versus *fear.*

Here is a charming example of how universal and independent of racial cultures are these story types. The inhabitants of the Trobriand Islands—tiny South Sea specks of land off the coast of New Guinea—are primitive Papuo-Melanesians. Certainly they cannot be suspected of any Western European literary roots. Yet here is the Greek legend of Daedalus and Icarus, South Sea Island style. The story is reported by the noted anthropologist, Bronislaw Malinowski, in his *Magic, Science, and Religion, and Other Essays* (Free Press, Glencoe, Ill., 1949).

An ambitious louse, desiring to see some of the neighboring islands, makes a deal with a butterfly to ferry him over. Midway the louse looks down at the sea below and is suddenly overcome with fear. He screams, the startled butterfly jerks, and the louse falls off and is drowned.

Type A, happy ending: "Neawtha's Warpath." *Arapaho Indian folk tale.*

I-nitial character: Neawtha.

Problem: Laziness versus *ambition.*

Here is another amusing folk tale, this time from the Arapaho Indians of North America. They also can hardly be said to have been influenced by any European literary tradition. Yet here again is the "Type A, happy-ending" pattern.

Neawtha, a very lazy Indian, lies abed while a war party steals out afoot to find and plunder an enemy village. After a while he gets up, mounts his pony, and circles ahead of the war party to have a campfire and a meal waiting for them when they arrive, footsore and weary, at dusk. He does this several times, always riding his pony, doing it the easy way while the others walk. When they arrive in the enemy country, they find and lose the trail of an enemy village. The others search for the trail while Neawtha sleeps. The others find no trace. But Neawtha asks an ant that happens to be crawling over him. Following the ant back to his nest, he finds tracks there which tell him the village went west.

The war party finds the village. The warriors decide to attack the camp from the other side. Neawtha is too lazy to go along, so he stays where he is. When the warriors attack the Indians in the village, all rush to the other end of the camp to repel the assault. Neawtha calmly walks into the abandoned tipis, gathers up the loot, unties the ponies tethered near by, and rides off, loaded down with plunder. On the way back home he meets his companions, defeated and running from the enemy. He gives them rides on his captured ponies.

Neawtha ties himself on his pony so he can sleep as they go home. The others can lead him in. He has demonstrated that laziness profits more than ambition.

This story was first printed in *Folk-Say: A regional miscellany*, edited by B. A. Botkin for the Oklahoma Folk-lore Society (University of Oklahoma Press, Norman, Okla., 1929), and is quoted by Stanley Vestal in his *Short Grass Country*. It is typically Indian in that the emotion which whites would normally consider "wrong," viz., laziness, is here the "right" choice, leading the hero to a reward.

The folk tales and stories of all other nations will be found to display these same three types. Sometimes they do not agree, as here, on which emotion is the "right" one and which is the "wrong." But the pattern of two emotions, conflicting in the same breast, the necessity for a final choice between them, the sacrificial nature of the decision, and the twist which, surprisingly, produces a reward where one would expect a loss, or, in the "Type B, unhappy endings," a loss where logically one anticipates a reward, is always evident.

The backward literary story is also to be found in nearly all folk cultures.

The important thing here is to distinguish between the pattern which is universal and the particular application which may vary infinitely. Thus laziness was a virtue, a "right" emotion for the Arapaho Indian. For the classically oriented white man it would be a vice, a "wrong" emotion. But the necessity for a choice between right and wrong and the twist after the choice, the reversal, are the same in both the Indian and the white story. Or for a more familiar example in a story involving the problem of *love* versus *honor*, ordinarily if the hero is the principal character, his "right" choice will be honor. But if the story is the heroine's, her "right" choice will usually be love. Women are just differently oriented than men.

You must learn to see this pattern. Do not let the materials or the particular application confuse you. The pattern is always the same. It has three variations: happy ending, unhappy ending, and backwards. Once you have mastered these three types, you will be able to recognize them in all the stories mankind tells. There are, it is true, amorphous jumbles currently passing for fiction, and in our confused age it does seem there is an unusual volume of such trash. But about this you need not worry. It has nothing to teach you. Over the centuries the stories that have endured all show, partially or wholly, some one of the three types here given.

CHAPTER VI

Character

CHARACTER IS THE objective aspect of conflict. Thus a battle-field will have character because it retains the signs of the struggle that took place on it. Conflict creates character. But only after it has been created do we have the signs, the evidences, that we identify as characteristics. This distinction needs to be noted very carefully.

In a plot or story we will have a character facing a problem. Always we try to make the problem fit the character and vice versa. We can illustrate this, perhaps, in the testing of a sword blade.

When the smith makes the blade, he tries to incorporate into it contradictory characteristics. It must be stiff enough to penetrate and yet flexible enough to bend. It must be hard enough to take a sharp edge, to cut, and yet malleable enough not to break or chip. Stiffness and flexibility, hardness and softness—these are contradictory. You cannot have 100 per cent of both in the same object. And yet this is precisely the problem the smith faces.

When he has done his best and produced a blade, it is tested. We may call the blade the character. The testing is the plot. The blade is thrust against a solid block of oak, to see what happens. If the point penetrates and does not blunt, if the blade bends but does not break, if it springs back straight when withdrawn, it has passed this part of the test. The edge is struck forcibly against something hard. If it cuts but does not break or chip, again it passes the test. Thrust against something it cannot penetrate, struck against something it cannot cut, it still must not break or bend permanently. If it endures all these indignities, it has passed the test.

A good story shows the same features. The principal character will be a combination of contradictory characteristics. They conflict inside of him just as the contradictions are forged into the sword blade. The plot then puts him up against a test to see how well the contradictions have been fused, to learn if the right characteristics, the right emotion, will prevail in the crisis. If the blade cannot penetrate, it must not break, or bend permanently. If it cannot cut, it must not chip or shatter. Just so, also, with our human character.

Now what this means, as an aside, in the conception of a character, is that virtually always we imagine him with a past. Something has happened to him to give him characteristics, to make him a capital character, before he appears in our first paragraph. Sometimes we tell these past happenings in the story, sometimes we do not. But always in what he does, in how he acts, he shows these characteristics. We know he is a sword blade, and we know also the test will be thrust and cut. We do not test a sword blade by trying to run it through a cream separator.

The principal character and the plot must be apropos; they must match.

You will notice this gives you two ways to arrive at a story. You can begin with the character and supply an appropriate plot. Or you can begin with the plot and provide a fitting character.

Stories for the young ordinarily are action stories in which the real character is more or less being forged in the action, to emerge complete only at the end. The more mature your reader audience, the more likely it is that they will prefer character stories, tales in which the hero or heroine's character is already virtually complete and the action is primarily a testing, a reaffirmation, of something we are pretty sure about from the start. In this sort of story the plot action will typically be much less violent than in the youthful action story.

The difficult point to master about character creating is in combining truly contradictory characteristics. Usually we can easily recognize one trait, one emotion, as strength. But all too often the other, which must first conflict and then combine with it, seems to us weakness. As we begin to put a character together, it is always best to ask ourselves what we would consider the weak aspects of such a man. What would we deem his faults? Quite ordinarily these faults or weaknesses turn out to be the opposite emotion, the strengths in other directions that complete the character.

Thus, as classic examples, Theodore Roosevelt, the famous exponent of the strenuous life, was a weakling in his youth and overcame all sorts of physical difficulties by sheer force of will. His "tags," if you are old enough to remember, his characteristic features that universally appeared in every cartoon or picture, were strong, gleaming, animal teeth, vitality exemplified, and eyeglasses, crutches for weak eyes!

Weakness and strength were set together in the sign manual that meant T. R. And his famous dictum, "Speak softly and carry a big stick," was another example of the same coupling. Notice that obvious force was not set against force, nor weakness against weakness.

Franklin D. Roosevelt, with his crippled body, his clear, strong, unfaltering voice, and his will and manner that contradicted all the weaknesses of his physical make-up, was another illustration of the same coupling. And to cite an immortal example from fiction, also, Robert Louis Stevenson's Dr. Jekyll and Mr. Hyde, the same character with one gentle, benevolent side and one blackly malevolent side, is yet another such pairing.

Ordinarily in learning characterization one will begin

with recognized examples. Such and such a person, we say
to ourselves, is a character. We do not realize quite why.
Usually we see only one side of the contradiction, the reversal (for such *character* really is), and only sense the other
side. But to create such characters on paper, or even to re-
produce them satisfactorily, we must learn to see the other
side also. A good trick here is to get in the habit of inverting
all the real characters one recognizes. Thus we ask ourselves,
what would Franklin D. Roosevelt have been had not polio
struck him down? Suppose Theodore Roosevelt had possessed good eyes and a normal healthy body? Would he
have had the driving urge to become a Rough Rider, to
charge up San Juan Hill, or to become our most strenuous
president? The answer, of course, is no, and thus by inverting we can see that a seeming weakness actually was a source
of strength, an apparent frailty, a virtue.

All of the great characters of history will be found to
have possessed these contradictions. Napoleon was a little
man and also possibly an epileptic. Small stature has probably produced more giants, particularly in business, than
any other single physical feature. Julius Caesar was an epileptic. Beethoven was deaf. Edgar Allen Poe was a drunkard
and a melancholic. Ulysses S. Grant was a drunkard and a
failure until President Lincoln discovered him and wished
he could send a barrel of Grant's whisky to his other gen-
erals. Charles Proteus Steinmetz, the electrical wizard who
perhaps did more to strengthen labor's hand than any other
man, was a hunchback. And so it goes all through the records.

The current advertising slogan, "Tough, but oh so gentle," is another application of the same principle. You learn
to apply it deliberately in character creation.

Suppose, for instance, we want to make a memorable
Western marshal. We expect him to be brave, tough, enduring, but with what shall we contrast these qualities to bring
out his character? Why, we shall make him loving, gentle,

perhaps even fearful of some particular thing. And we shall remember to put physical signs of these contradictions in our description of him. He has broad shoulders but a soft voice, or steel gray eyes but gentle hands. And we remember to parade these tags, setting one against the other all through the story.

Or perhaps we want a heroine—gentle, soft, and feminine. How do we bring these out? We give her a whim of iron. When she sets her mind to something, nothing can change her. Her mouth is sweet and soft and curved, but her square little finger tips are those of a doer. And again we parade these conflicting tags all through the story.

What kind of a plot would we use for such a character? Very likely, it should be a *love* versus *ambition* plot in which our little girl has a driving urge to keep papa's newspaper on its feet, or operate a successful oil company, or maybe just run the cow ranch Uncle has left her. But the hero, on the neighboring ranch, say, appears to be a cattle rustler. If she succeeds with the ranch, she must ruthlessly get rid of the hero. She starts in to do so. But when she discovers the other ranchers in the area have decided to lynch our hero and are about to swing him from a convenient limb, love conquers all and she rushes to the rescue and saves him, even though she is convinced he has been stealing her cattle.

In the scene where she is saving our hero's neck, the leader of the lynching party protests a little too violently. He and the hero have a fight. The lynch leader's shirt gets torn off, or he goes for a hidden gun, or something. Anyway, suddenly he is revealed as the real cattle thief. So our heroine saves both her love and her ranch by choosing, seemingly, to sacrifice all for love.

What sort of characterizations would we use for the heroine? Well, we have given her a sweet mouth for the feminine, lovable tag, and square finger tips for the business trait. These are physical tags. She would also have mannerisms, habits of speech or action, which would display the same emotions. Thus, we could make her very crisp in her way of speaking, except when she sees a baby, a tiny colt, or a calf. Then she is very soft and anything but crisply businesslike. We could place the same emotions in her past: she has successfully operated a store in town, but all the children adored her because she was always giving them candy and taking time out to hear their small troubles. And we can work in incidents in the story showing the same feelings: she rides out in a storm to fix a fence and mends it very efficiently herself. But then on the way back she stops to pick up and bring in a meadow lark that has broken its leg. She nurses the bird back to health and he stays around the ranch. Or, to make this an even better symbol, perhaps it is a hawk that she picks up and nurses. He is "mean as all git out" to everybody else, but he loves her; he hangs around the ranch house and she can do anything with him.

You may, if you wish, assemble a character as you might some kind of a machine, deciding first what conflicting emotions have gone together to make the personality, then cold-bloodedly providing the double tags of physical traits, mannerisms, habits of speech or action, and so on. It is probably good practice to try this a few times until you are familiar with the way the pieces go together. But in my experience, almost never will a writer achieve a very good character by such mechanical operation.

On the contrary, nearly all good characters come to the writer, rather than being deliberately assembled by him. The author does not think them up; he dreams them up instead. Consciously, or unconsciously, the characters are assembled from people he has known or has heard or read about. But proper digestion is ordinarily an unconscious function. When you try to do it by the numbers, as some writing texts advocate, nearly always you come up with a robot, a creaking, lifeless character.

It is good practice to keep a notebook and set down every character that catches your interest, whether you ever use him, or her, or not. On the street, at business, in meetings, parties, anywhere and everywhere, you meet usable characters. The great difficulty you will have to overcome is a sort of spiritual blindness that keeps you from seeing just what makes them interesting, what makes them characters. If you can teach yourself the habit of quick diagnosis and analysis after you have sensed that here is a character, you will have given yourself an invaluable tool not only for writing but also for business and social contacts. Being able to judge the other fellow quickly and accurately is the first great step toward success. It is as important in direct contact with other people as it is in discovering good fictional material.

Learn to look for the tangible expression of the conflicting emotions—the placid eyes and the nervous, ever-moving hands; the immaculate dress and the run-over heels; the marshal's star on the vest and the sack of stick candy for the kids in the coat pocket. Always, when you discover a real character, you will find also these evidences of the rival emotions. Look for them and write them down. It is quite likely you will never use the notes, but the act of seeing them, the operation of writing them down, will establish the habit of thought that you are after.

There are two basic types of characters—the subjectively oriented, and the objectively oriented, varieties. A very simple test usually can distinguish one from the other for you if you can find the opportunity to try it. Merely have the subject point at some small object across the room —point from the hip, so to speak, without taking deliberate aim. Then ask him to close one eye, then the other, and see which eye lines up with the pointing finger.

If right hand, right eye, or left hand, left eye, correspond, the subject is probably objective in his approach. He is a type that will listen to what you have to say and remember at least part of it. If you are trying to tell him how to do something, trying to teach him, you will find that he is receptive. But he very seldom adds anything to what you tell him, and ordinarily he will have difficulties in beginning.

This has proven true in about 85 per cent of the writing students I have coached over the years. A linear-minded, objective student will usually see the end of a story quite clearly, but he will have difficulty with his beginnings. He is, in short, like a farsighted person, who can read if his arms are long enough but who has all sorts of trouble with print close up.

Something less than half of the people you meet, however, will be another breed of cat. They will point with their right finger but left eye. Or they will use their left hand and right eye. Such cross-visioned individuals almost invariably are subjectively oriented. You cannot tell them anything. They will listen to nothing. They will do nothing you tell them to do, but, on the contrary, if they do anything, will try the opposite. Such people must be handled in exactly the reverse fashion from that useful for objective characters.

You never tell a subjective character anything you want him to know. Instead, you ask him to tell you. You instruct him by listening to him, not by talking. And why our schools of education have not long since discovered this fundamental difference in human personalities I do not know. But teachers, unconsciously at least, have applied it for hundreds of years.

Any good classroom will show an alternation of lecture and recitation—one period in which the teacher tells the pupils, another in which the pupils tell the teacher. The primary purpose of this is not to see if the students "remember," as most people imagine. Instead, it is a practical application to a mixed group of the lecture and Socratic methods.

Two thousands years ago the great Greek philosopher, Socrates, confronted with a highly subjective, very creative group of students, developed the method of instructing by asking, not telling. Probably somewhat more than half of those who listened to him gained nothing at all from the great philosopher, but instead gleaned whatever grains they did from the answers of the students. You will remember that we read Plato and Xenophon to find out what Socrates taught; and how much of the printed thought is Socrates', and how much Plato's and Xenophon's, no one knows. But both the subjective and the objective minds in Socrates' impromptu classes, we know, did profit—the one from answering questions and seeing for themselves in their own first persons, the others from listening, remembering, and seeing in third person. When you as a writer are creating a character, it is best to know first just what kind of a character you yourself possess, and then decide what sort you are creating—objective or subjective.

Most of the current psychologies and psychiatric textbooks, at least those intended for popular use, are very misleading in that the authors never clearly distinguish between objective and subjective characters. They are like the inhabitants of biblical Nineveh, to whom the prophet Jonah was sent. They cannot tell their right hand from their left. Now this is so simple that it is difficult to see on first reading. But presently (I hope!) it will become self evident, as you study that there are two diametrically different kinds of human character.

When we look in a mirror and see our reflection, that is the only place in this world that we will ever consciously see ourselves. We know that the real face is in front of the mirror and that the reflection looking back is only an image. But we shall never see the real face directly. Accordingly, it is very easy to slip into the habit of thought that makes the image the reality or beginning place. We forget or ignore the fact that the reflection is reversal, and we start doing things backwards.

Now this is precisely the thing that religion thunders against and that is specifically prohibited in the first commandment. Not only are graven images banned as beginning points—"Thou shalt have no other Gods before me." This is primarily a grammatical injunction. It establishes the supremacy of the first person, that "I" or "me" that I shall never directly see. Nevertheless, in this irreligious age, we have fallen again into the habit of considering the objective to be superior, beginning from the image, now object, rather than the subject.

As we have noted, something more than half of an average group will have minds that work this way, from the image back toward themselves. A minority will have minds that work from the observing first person, the "I" "me," or "my," out toward the object or image. This means that we have traffic coming and traffic going in any group, and we shall never be able to satisfy them all with any one story or character.

But in a good story we will have at least one subjective character and always a number of objective ones. So perhaps if a reader does not prefer the one, he will like some of the others. Typically nowadays, if the hero is subjective, the heroine is objective, or vice versa. And once again, just what do I mean by this?

Well, suppose our hero is a strong, silent man who talks only by doing, who "went thataway" all by himself. He is the lone cowboy, the one ranger, the solo marshal, the rugged individualist. We know immediately, he is subjective. The heroine? She'll be the community schoolteacher— talkative, gregarious, and essentially objective.

Perhaps we should repeat here what we have said in other words about basic character. It depends altogether on how one sees one's world, or oneself. Until our times, the heroes in stories almost without exception have been rugged individualists, singular souls who considered themselves distinct and apart from the common herd. It was not their ambition to attain security by making themselves just another Model T. But in our troubled age, with its inversion of values, the opposite sort of character begins to be heroized. And this is confusing.

But let's stick to fundamentals. A subjective character begins from some sort of intangible ego, some ineffable "I" deep within himself. He thinks confession-style, in first person. He knows and believes only what he sees for himself. If his drive extends out beyond his own body, he is a creative, or at least an active, personality. Like Faust, he is always on the move or he perishes. He speaks in terms of action, and he may be a bold marshal, an outlaw, a gangster, or a fighter pilot—always something where there is motion.

If his drive does not extend beyond his own person, he will be a Narcissus type, always admiring himself, a clothes horse, a primper; or if this is a feminine character, she will be clothes and cosmetics crazy.

Notice that this sort of character is the opposite of the objectively oriented individual whose drive is similarly confined to his own body. The objective type, seeking to draw objects in, rather than direct energy out, will be a glutton, a miser, or a hog. Most psychologies fail completely to distinguish between these two, calling both inverts.

Neither, in extreme form, makes a good fictional character, save as a villain. Fictional characters, to be interesting, must have a drive that reaches out beyond their own bodies. They must be interested in others, either for others' sake or for their own purposes. And once again, although what they do may seem similar, the ultimate effects are directly opposite.

Thus, a minister, priest, or rabbi endeavoring to serve a member of his congregation is doing so for the sake of the member. He is trying to help another person for that other person's benefit. But a cattle rancher, fattening a cow or saving her from the wolves, is doing so for his own benefit. Presently he will drive that cow to the slaughterhouse and pocket her price for his profit. The rescue actions appear similar, but they are for directly opposite purposes.

You should be sure for what ultimate purpose your character is performing a given action when you set out to put him down on paper; and, certainly, in recognizing characters in real life, in trying to analyze them, you should always try to project to that ultimate goal. What's he doing it for? And here we have our finger on the secret of genuine character.

Unknowingly, at least to begin, the truly great subjective character sees himself in the people around him. At first he rejects this because he feels that he is separate and distinct from them, that he is different. But at the character-creating crisis he obeys the inner intuition, he does something which he thinks is entirely for the benefit of someone else. He discovers, to his amazement, that his action has been for his own benefit, that the "other" person is himself. This is the basis of plot, and, to say it again, character is nothing in the world but the objective aspects of plot; character is the sign left by a story that has happened.

We forge the sword blade, and we try to incorporate in it contradictory characteristics. It must be stiff yet flexible. It must be hard and still not brittle. We do the best we can and then we put it to the test. We see if it will penetrate and not break, if it will bend but spring back straight, if it will cut and not nick. If it passes the test, then it has character. If it fails, it has lost character. It is no longer a sword but only broken pieces of metal.

CHAPTER VII

The Ingredients: Sin, Sex, and Science

IN THIS OBJECTIVE AGE with its worship of other gods the precepts of our fathers, unfortunately, all too often no longer make sense. They were addressed to generations who spoke a language other than ours. In this chapter we are going to try to translate some of these principles, to show that they continue to be as valid and practical as ever.

It will help you to understand what we have to say now if you are of a religious bent. But you do not need to be. Doubtless you will grant that there must be something practical, something worth while, about religion, or it would not be found in all times and all places. Plainly, some people do get something from it. Just what this something is, in its practical applications, is what we are trying to consider here.

If you will examine any moral precept, you will discover that invariably it resembles a road sign, a traffic direction. It says, in effect, "Stop," "Go," "Keep to the Right," "Bridge out Ahead," or the like. That is, it tells you how to proceed in the immediate future, what to do and which way to go "next." It is the same sort of thing you run into when you go somewhere on a motor trip. The filling station men, the tourist aids, will tell you about the road ahead, advise you on right and wrong courses. Just so with morals.

It is fairly evident that we are imperfect minds living in a creation far more complex than we can grasp. The legend of the rainbow in the Bible, and in the mythologies of many other people as well, is an intriguing illustration of this. Probably what it means is that the generations before Noah (or whoever the first man was who saw a rainbow) were color blind. One has to have three points in his eyes, three intangible factors, to be able to see color. What this probably means is that color vision requires three-dimensional perception, ability to see in depth, and color-blind persons or animals probably see principally in two dimensions.

The first man to see in true perspective, in three dimensions, lifting his eyes, saw the first rainbow. It impressed him so much that it has been in man's legends ever since.

Now we know, pretty definitely, that there is at least one more special dimension, and perhaps there are many more. But of the fourth dimension, anyhow, we are pretty sure. It is what we call "time." Time is a mysterious sort of space in which we are moved but cannot move of our own free will. Which gives us the hint as to just where we are in the mastery of it.

We have the objective, but not the subjective, ends of the thing. It can push us around. But we have not yet learned how to push it. Except—and here is where moralities come in:

Imagine this is a daily journey around the block. With the conscious mind capable of handling only three dimensions, three sides of the block, we are up against a tall dilemma when we get to the fourth side. We are required to go all the way around, but we are forbidden to see or know anything about that fourth side. How can both requirements be obeyed?

Well, we can have ourselves put to sleep, or drugged, and carried down the fourth side on each round. And you will notice this is exactly what we do each day. From two-thirds to three-fourths of our day we spend in conscious, waking activities, handling the three dimensions we can see. But the fourth part of the day we sleep, and no physiologist can explain why.

You do not have to rest a clock or a motor six to eight hours out of every day, and as a matter of demonstrated fact the body does not rest either during sleep. Some of its activities go on at an accelerated pace, and all of them continue—even motion. Only consciousness, that is the awareness of the relationship of one's body to the things around it, is suspended. We cannot say that this demonstrates the existence of a fourth dimension. But we can guess pretty shrewdly that this is the explanation of sleep. It is nature's way of adapting us to a world of which we can handle only a part.

What about that fourth part, the portion our conscious minds are not permitted to enter? We have to live through, pass through, that, too. Nor is it only when we are in bed asleep that we must somehow deal with it. We sleep in brief snatches, intervals, perhaps only a second or two at a time, all during our waking hours also. This is the explanation for many automobile wrecks. The drivers merely go to sleep at the wheel for one brief wink in broad daylight. It is just for a second but the second is fatal. And all of us know that there are times and days when we will cat nap for long minutes, perhaps bolt upright, perhaps keeping right on at whatever we are doing.

How then does one get safely through these dark periods, either the long sleep at night, or the many brief black instants during the day? Here is where morality applies.

Moral precepts are traffic directions, and they are normally pounded into the individual, repeated over and over and over, indoctrinated across years of space, until they literally become almost second nature. The idea is to make them as nearly automatic as we can. Then in the instant of darkness and stress the individual will automatically do the right thing, do it before he can wake up to think.

And you will notice here that we are talking about the pattern of story.

In the middle of the black moment, at the point of decision and sacrifice, the story hero acts automatically, on some basis other than that of conscious thought. Usually he does the opposite of that which logic and self-interest would dictate. The story is about a succession of incidents in time, that is, a trip, a journey, including a point of no return. And a journey needs road maps and directions.

People who are primarily agricultural, or who are nomads, such as sheepmen and cattle ranchers, know this basic truth intuitively. They do not have to be told that a man on his own needs a compass somewhere inside himself. They actually have such an ability.

It was my good fortune to be born and reared on the last American frontier and to have known many frontiersmen, cowboys, Indians, soldiers, and old-timers. One of their most striking characteristics was this sense of direction.

They needed no street signs, no traffic cops or highway markers. They knew where they were "at" always. Set them down anywhere, at any time, in a strange surrounding however confusing, and they could orient themselves. By some means as mysterious as that which guides the wild goose, or the salmon or eel at sea, they knew their directions and they knew their way. They could not tell how they knew; they just did.

I have noticed also that this quality is strikingly absent in a great many of the inhabitants of big cities. They do not know north from south, or east from west. A surprising number are like the citizens of Biblical Nineveh, not even knowing their right hand from their left. To such people there is no directional reality, and of course it is impossible to tell them so.

But, fortunately, most of us, even in the great cities, still possess at least some rudiments of orientation, some potential ability to feel our proper way. This, as we have noticed at length in the preceding chapters, is the underlying secret of plot and story. Now suppose we look at the religious application.

Perhaps your Sunday-school teacher did not call it to your attention. But you will remember that both Father Abraham and Moses, the great lawgiver, were trail drivers, cattlemen, and sheepmen. In their time and place they faced the same necessities, the same requirements, as our own American pioneers, our emigrants to Oregon and California, our cattlemen, and our Texas trail drivers. These requirements they met in their own ways and languages. Moses, educated in the priestly schools of Egypt, undoubtedly knew the great royal secret of that ancient land. There were two religions—one for the common herd, objective, pluralistic and collective, designed primarily to keep the commoner a contented cow; and the other for the priests and Pharoah, a monotheism which is the directional ability a leader must have to succeed.

When the iconoclastic Pharoah, Amenhotep IV, tried to introduce this secret faith—the exclusive worship of Aten, symbolized by the sun disk—as a popular one, he was soon beaten down, and the old pluralistic religion was restored. The Israelites were in Egypt at this time, and it was under the next dynasty, the nineteenth, that Moses led them out of bondage.

Now without any intended irreverence, practically speaking, what did Moses have that made him a leader? That God gave him certain qualities is beside the point. Of course God did. But can we understand what they were and how he used them?

You need to realize first that God is the name for the beginning point, the prime landmark in any classic scheme of things. In our irreligious age, we find it hard to realize that a property stake could be endowed with mystic powers. And indeed the ancient had the same difficulty, hopelessly confusing himself on the distinction between the arithmetic and the apples, the intangible pattern of reality and the tangible symbols which imperfect man must use to enwrap and outline the pattern so that he may see it.

But the problem of Moses was the problem of a navigator, an explorer, or a land surveyor. He had to lead a people unerringly through an uncharted wilderness to a given destination, the Promised Land.

He had no compass, no sextant, no navigator's instruments. So his compass had to be inside of himself. And to be accurately usable over long distances, it must respond only to one magnetic field, one beginning point, one north pole.

Villagers, living their lives in one locality, never getting out of sight of the village temple, might get along with many idols, gods, beginning points. They aren't going anywhere anyhow, so it doesn't matter. But for a traveler with a north pole in every hamlet he passes, and dozens of them in each city, this could be dreadfully confusing. He would never know to which local beginning point, which nearest god, his compass was pointing. He could set no true course to anywhere beyond his immediate range of vision.

Which, of course, was the reason the ancient ruler gave his people a pluralistic religion, while, if he were wise, he kept a monotheism for himself.

Knowing nothing of compasses and navigation, possessing not one word of a modern traveler's vocabulary, Moses necessarily had to speak to his people in the words they could understand, those of religion. But when we look at what he did and read the language of reality, rather than the temporal words, we can know what his powers were. He knew his way just as one of our own Texas trail drivers, heading north with a longhorn herd, knew his. And that is not irreverent in either case. Who made the earth to have a magnetic field, to have directions—north and south and east and west—and Who taught His creatures to sense and to use them, if not the Creator?

93

This practical necessity for just one north pole Moses phrased religiously as one God. And even though they often fell from grace, still it is to the glory of the ancient Israelites that they never quite lost sight of the guiding concept. They have made their way successfully across the millenniums, they have even gone home again, because they clung to one north pole. This same sense of direction, for practical purposes, is our story sense.

To violate this sense of direction is to sin. To obey it is to retain virtue. With obvious connection to the directions, the ancient moralist Plato distinguished four cardinal virtues—prudence, fortitude, temperance, and justice. Calling these the natural virtues, Christian moralists, discarding the backward way as their faith demanded, set up a triad—faith, hope, and charity—as the supernatural or Christian virtues. You will observe that the Platonian virtues are mainly oriented to the past, while the Christian virtues are all qualities directed blindly toward an unknown, unseen, future end. The orientations are directly opposite.

Now plots and stories endeavor to illustrate the use of this directional intuition. In the form of a parable they try to show the reader how he, too, should go in a similar situation. When he comes to his fourth side, his black interval, here, they say, is the way to drive safely through it. And if some of us are going to insist on looking backward while we try the feat, others forward, naturally we are going to differ considerably in our explanations of how to turn the trick.

We shall probably use the same symbols, the same markers. But one set of us will be in effect going, while the others, like the images in a mirror, are in appearance coming. Lots of room to get oneself mystified!

We can set down these fundamentals, however, and perhaps puzzle out our way. The basis of the so-called "unity" of a story is this use of one north pole, one guideline, one morality, one story line, to hold the tale intact. The hero holds rigidly to the "right" course, even through the black moment. And by such navigation he emerges happily on the other side. Or he fails to hold straight on his course and lets himself be deflected. Then he emerges unhappily.

Or, finally, like reflections in a mirror, he knows no real direction, no actual coming or going. He believes himself to be doing everything backwards. And in the end (poor "literary" tragedy) he discovers he is nothing and has got nowhere.

In human life itself, the great beginning points are birth and death. About the other sides of these we can only speculate. It is a curious fact that we do not even know the length of pregnancy of a human being but can only guess and approximate it, often missing our guess by weeks. And this despite the experience of billions and billions of births! About death we have nothing save hope to offer. But midcourse in life we have another north pole we can use, a sort of equator. This is sex.

Here is the basic reason most stories concern themselves with love, or at least have a romantic element. The act of sex all but the most primitive peoples have long since recognized as a true beginning or ending point of some sort, either a goal toward which the journey may be directed, or a port from which the voyage is begun.

A subjectively oriented people, looking toward the future, will consider sex as a taboo subject. They will endeavor to begin their picture of reality with a virgin birth, a creation that does not have behind it the sex act which they know forms a continuation of the earthly chain. This concept of a virgin-birth beginning and this regard of sex as forbidden, taboo, will be found not only in the Christian faith but in other subjectively oriented religions as well.

An objectively oriented people will consider sex as the totem, the goal. Birth and even children tend to become more or less taboo topics. But the sex act itself and events leading up to it will be treated in great detail. Conversely, in a story directed to a subjective, essentially religious-minded audience, we will have little or no sex, scant physical description of the bodily charms of the heroine, and instead a great deal of wordage spent on the motion, the movement, right or wrong, of a character.

The classic Western story is a typical example of subjective treatment. It devotes itself to the struggles of the cowman trying to get his trail herd through the hostile Indians, or of the marshal seeking to pacify a lawless town. Sex acts play no part in it, and the women, for the most part, are angels waiting in the wings to come down at the end with heaven's rewards. You kiss your horse instead of your girl at the windup of a Western.

To an objectively minded audience this is foolishness. Instead, to them, typically, a woman is an object to be pursued as the goal of the story. The sexual act itself is not in forbidden territory and will quite often be described in nauseating detail. But what follows in due period thereafter—a baby and parenthood—these are for the most part very carefully ignored.

In the first plot, sex is the intangible element, not put into words, though often very strongly present. In the second, the objective story, sex is the tangible element, set down in words. It is, I mean, either totem or taboo, depending upon what kind of story we are writing, which way we are going. And it is not possible to go both ways at the same time.

Before science, there was magic. Both are very old, but magic is the older. And these we need to understand also, because plots and stories can be written on their patterns, which will differ from what we have just described as journeys east and west differ from travels north and south.

Science is the recognition of the orderly relationship of objects to objects, objective aspects to objective aspects, objective happenings to objective happenings. All of these must root in the past. This is not merely because we see objects and objective aspects only in hindsight. It is also a requirement of scientific dogma. A fact, to be recognized as such, must recur. It must have happened before, and it must have happened not once but many times, before the scientist will admit it to his book of demonstrated fact. Thus committed to looking backward, science, as the great scientists freely admit, has no regard for, or consideration of, the future. It has no morality and no more use for it than a reflection in the mirror would have for a compass. Its direction is two dimensional, from side to side. Which is the confusing part.

But to try at least to illustrate, it says in effect that when you hold two apples of equal size side by side at equal distances from a mirror, the images will be equal in size. The apples are objects, ranged in order from right to left, and the images are similarly flat. The instant at which we perceive them they are in the past, in hindsight. This is another possibly confusing point.

We have been taught that light rays bring to us all that we see and that these rays travel in finite time. When we look at a star, for an extreme example, we believe that we do not see the star as it is "now." Instead, we see it as it was years and perhaps centuries ago. During all that time, so we have been told, the light rays, like a freight train, have been bringing the images to us, so that "now" if we should see the star flicker or explode we could do nothing about it, even if we had supernatural powers. We could do nothing because it happened centuries ago, you understand, and to think we could do anything "now" would be like proposing to undo the American Revolution, or have the South win the Battle of Gettysburg.

97

Now the strange truth is that subjectively oriented people do not see reality, see their world, in this way at all. Instead, they look from themselves toward the future. They see no images, no objects, in the future, and this is why graven images are forbidden by the great religions. But they, also, are subject to this side-to-side diversion. And for them it is magic.

When a subjectively oriented individual goes to a witch doctor or a wizard for a love potion, or perhaps for a medicine to cause the death of an enemy, he is trying to match a subjective future state with an objective future state.

That is, he wants the beloved person "tomorrow" to be in love with him. Or he wishes the hated individual to be dead "tomorrow." Thus magic is the subjective side of science, and science is the objective, hindsight aspect, of magic. Each hates and fears the other. And yet continually what was magic yesterday has become science today. Astrology turns into astronomy, alchemy into chemistry, the supernatural into the natural. We can write stories about these also if we wish.

The detective story, at least in its classic version where the Sherlock Holmes hero triumphantly solves the mystery by relating the accomplished crime to some tangible objective clue left by the criminal, is simply the scientific method exemplified in a parable. We can, of course, write detective stories in which romantic elements—love, sex, or any or all of the other materials of fiction—enter in. But basically the detective-story fan is flat-minded. His is a visual world. He wants to see an object related to an object, or an objective aspect to an objective aspect. He desires a triumph of the intellect. Only incidentally does the fact that a discovery of a crime and detection of the criminal aid justice and morality enter into the concept. The punishment of the criminal is usually placed as a sort of postscript to the story, if it is given at all.

Stories of magic and fantasy—of the Sleeping Beauty who can be awakened to love the handsome prince, or of the magic wand which "tomorrow" may bring together the wish and the wisher—have very little place in our objective world. They can be written for children, but they primarily are tales for simple, primitive, or youthful minds. They bring scant reward on today's market.

The science-fiction story is essentially the detective story, or an effort to write fantasy, the magical or fairy tale, in objective terms. Equip Jack with a super plant-food, give the beanstalk a scientific name, and make the giant an inhabitant of an unknown planet in outer space, and you have transformed the familiar fairy story into quite acceptable science fiction. Its audience appears to be limited largely to those who in previous ages would have read fairy stories. Which is not to say it is composed altogether of the young.

In a normal forward story, the twist at the climax, the unexpected answer or reward, may very well be called a miracle. It is happening for the first time, at least in the experience of the VP character through whose eyes we are seeing it. It is surprising and wholly unexpected. Therefore it is not science or scientific. It is the very sort of thing science suspects and has taught its adherents to doubt until it has been demonstrated at least a few thousand times. This is why fiction does not flourish in a scientific age and why our current fiction is as pale, sickly, and unsatisfying as it is.

But the detective, the fact, the magical or science-fiction, side-to-side story, will not and cannot satisfy the innate human need for forward guides. An age without good fiction is a spiritually starved age. Nothing is more certain than that it will either eventually satisfy that need and replenish its fictional stocks, or it will perish. The great and enduring stories over the ages have all been of the forward, miracle type. They have been subjective. They have been essentially religious. It is something to remember.

99

CHAPTER VIII

The Anatomy of Story

WHAT WE HAVE to consider now is for the most part objective and fairly easy to grasp. This is the anatomy of story. It applies also to the novel and novelette, with appropriate length changes, but it is best seen in the short story. We do need to say something here, though, about the novel-length story whose form is a matter of great dispute in our times.

In our day a great many writers begin their careers with novels. Often, as beginners, they know little or nothing about story form. All too many of them would have no content to offer, even if they were taught the form. So many so-called novels are weird masses of confusion confounded, resembling nothing so much as the slime one finds on stagnant waters. They may perhaps be interesting to students of diseases. But the idea that story is a normal healthy organism about healthy characters and intended for healthy readers quite evades all too many writers and editors of our day.

Since this is not a work on parasitology, we will consider only the normal forms here. The form of the short story has emerged quite definitely, and normal novels also, including all of the great ones that have endured over the years, have a discernible plot form.

Sometimes because of the length of the work and because, also, a good deal of the technique is comparable to the chiaroscuro work of the pictorial artist, it is hard to pin point form in the novel. Because of his much greater canvas, the novelist can use lights and shadows, the haze of distance and so on, while the short-story writer must employ linear perspective, sharp lines, and often no more than a single line or two for his effect. But no matter; the desired goal is the same. We can see it here more simply in the short story.

The typical short story is between three thousand and five thousand words in length, with dwarf shorts on one extreme ranging down to as little as three hundred words, or even less. A joke, for that matter, perhaps no more than twenty to fifty words long, is in form a short story. On the other extreme are stories ranging up to perhaps seven thousand, or even eight thousand, words. But somewhere at about this range the ability of the average reader to follow the one story-line that distinguishes the true short story begins to fade, and by degrees we begin to move into the novelette field.

A novelette, typically, is two or more short stories woven together. It is usually from eight thousand to fifteen thousand words in length. Sometimes even a twenty-five-thousand-word story will be called a novelette. But ordinarily the magazine editors who buy most of the stories of this length will call this a novel. An actual book-length novel, of course, is a story in excess of fifty thousand words and can be as long as five hundred thousand words.

The true short story, twelve to eighteen pages long, divides into either three or four parts, depending upon its tempo and the times in which it is written. Now this is a subjective aspect which is apt to be confusing. But as a general thing, a changing age will tend to be triangular and spearheaded in its form, while a period more sure of itself will be square. The drill and tactical formations of the army are one mirror of this sort of change, as is the tempo of currently popular music.

You will remember, especially if you chance to be a veteran, that as the nation approached the uncertainties of World War II, the old square divisions, square squads, of

the army were abandoned in favor of triangular arrange-
ments, with a sort of follow-your-leader-no-matter-how-
many-of-you-there-are ordering of the men. It was a tactic
for muddled masses, a thoroughly unlovely arrangement,
except perhaps for bewildered sheep.

But the squads and divisions of an earlier day, when we
were more sure of ourselves, were square.

In its triangular form story has a beginning, a middle,
and an end. In its square form there are four parts. The
difference is usually that a distinction is made between the
actual performance of the decision and the realization of
it—making two parts where there was only one before. Now
let's follow a story through its four parts:

Part 1. This is about one-fourth of a story, typically the
first four pages. In this part the author must do the following things: set the stage, establish time and place, introduce
all the principal characters, characterize all the principal
characters, define the problem, begin the working out of the
problem, and finally bring in the first complication.

Part 2. This section, typically about four pages also,
begins with the first complication, which was introduced at
the end of Part 1. A first complication is a further difficulty
that arises from the opening problem but which is not an
inherent part of it. It serves to make the problem more difficult and complex. As an example, if our opening problem
is that mother-in-law is coming to visit the hero, a first complication could be that when she arrives he discovers she has
brought his seven mean little brothers-in-law and their pug-
nacious dog along with her. It was bad enough anticipating
mother-in-law. But mother-in-law, seven little monsters, and
a dog are much worse. The little monsters and the dog arrive
in the story because of mother-in-law's visit. But they were
not a part of the opening problem.

Sometimes this first complication is in itself enough to
carry the story through its middle. But usually additional

complications which arise from the previous problem or its complication are brought in. In contradiction to the way one would logically proceed, story-plot solves its problems by trying to make matters as difficult as possible. If one can make the problem wholly insoluble and completely unbearable, then a solution is easy. The blackest black can always be reversed into pure white. It is the muddy grays that give trouble. Turn them over and they are apt to be gray mud.

The distinction between Part 3 and Part 4 is the place where one may have trouble. In a three-part-division story the decision and sacrifice ordinarily come in one packet at the end of Part 2. Part 3 is devoted to the reward. But in a four-part division of story the actual performance of the sacrificial decision comes first—sometimes at the end of Part 2, but more typically during Part 3. Then several paragraphs, or perhaps even several pages, later, the conscious intellectual realization of what one has done is brought into the story. This usually ends Part 3 and introduces Part 4, the reward, or punishment.

In studying published stories, or in seeking faults in your own work, it is worth your while to try to break the story into its parts so that you may see its anatomical defects, if any. Outlining plots by parts is good practice also. But when it comes to the actual writing of a story, most writers will do better not to make and follow a detailed outline. The processes of creation and synthesis are entirely different from those of analysis. A story, like any other living thing, grows as a whole and not part-by-part. The anatomist dissects by parts. But when he is finished with his dissection, he never can put the pieces together again and endow them with life.

So dissect other people's stories to learn your plot anatomy, but have a respect for the life of your own. Let them alone, let them grow as a whole, and look at their parts only when you feel that there is something wrong with your brain child, that perhaps he should not really have two heads or sixteen feet.

The reason for this, of course, to say it in other words, is simply that anatomy is the backward look. No matter how skillfully written, a story that is planned ahead in detail and then written strictly according to plan will have a shopworn appearance, a slightly used, slightly dead, feel to it. To meet the birds or the butterflies where we placed them in the outline, we must kill them and string them on wires. The characters that strayed happily through our dreams as we thought the story up cannot be persuaded to come back in the formal writing. They will have to be chained down, clubbed, and hauled in, if we get them back at all, and thus beaten and manacled they are not the carefree characters we met in our dream.

So unless you are doing a very literary story, or a carefully calculated detective or mystery, do not outline your plot in detail ahead of time. You need only a beginning point and some landmark, some marker at the climax, to guide you. Perhaps it will be something someone does, right at the crisis—perhaps a gesture, a facial expression, possibly no more than a word or two that somehow seemed to fit right there. Begin your story and head for that point; let the parts develop as you go along. After you have written your first draft, then check its proportions, its parts, and see if you have approximated normal story-anatomy. You do not need to get it exact. The parts are merely a general guide. Many very fine stories are anatomically deformed. But again as a general thing the three- or four-part divisions of story serve as a guide to help you find out what is wrong when you sense that something has gone awry.

Most books on writing take the trouble to break stories into classes—action stories, character stories, mood, atmosphere, or whatnot. But it has always seemed to me that these are arbitrary and rather meaningless divisions, especially for the writer. The reader may like to classify what he reads into action stories, atmosphere tales, or the like, just as a casual observer of passing strollers may sort out the blonds, the short men, the tall ones, the fat, and the lean. But a mother going to have a baby does not say to herself, "I shall now have a tall, slim, dark football player," or perhaps, "a cute, small, vivacious blond." She finds it trouble enough merely to produce a baby and usually is quite content to take what comes. A baby is always a surprise. And so are good stories. No writer sitting down at his typewriter can be absolutely sure what will emerge. If he wishes to classify his work, he will do better to wait until the story has been produced before beginning his classification.

As we have noted in a previous chapter, the "literary" story is the reverse of the normal forward story, and its parts, when it has them, are similarly reversed. The story begins with what would normally be the end. The attempted decision and action comes next. It is usually very close to the beginning of the story, about four to six pages from the start. The remainder of the story, say ten to twelve pages, is then devoted to the hero's struggles with the backward complications, which bring him eventually to the problem which would open a normal story. But here, since he has backed into a dead-end street and does not know how to get out, we must leave him stuck forever on what would usually be an opening gambit. Or to say this more simply, in a literary plot the decision point is typically about one-fourth to one-third of the way through the story. In a normal story it comes about three-quarters of the way toward the end. The one sequence merely reverses the other.

Now here are some minor details of anatomy which you should know by eye as well as by ear. The most important is the *transition*.

No story can tell everything the hero does, not even in the brief space of time covered by the story. A great deal must be left out. And to get from the bit we use to the next piece we choose to include, we must use a connecting technique called a transition.

Unconsciously you use these between every sentence, every paragraph, that you write. But there will be spots where you will wish to crop out sizable chunks of space and time. Here is where the conscious transition comes in. It looks something like this:

"For a long moment he stared, grimly, then turned toward the door.

"And he was still grim when he came back in a week later."

You will notice that we have dropped out a whole week of the hero's life. But we have bridged the gap with an emotional cable. We have said that he was "grim" as he turned to go out and he was "still grim" when he came back in. This, with infinite variations, is the way all transitions are made.

The real story-line we are following is the emotional line, an intangible, only illustrated, or marked out, by the actions and objects we talk about in the story. If our hero was grim when he went out and still grim when he came back, then nothing has happened in the dropped interval to change the story-line. We do not need to tell anything that happened between his departure and his return.

But if something had happened during the week to change his mood drastically, then we should have told that incident, whatever it was. We can, if we wish, make a simple change in his emotional line. We can say he was grim as he went out, "but he felt a little better when he came back." We have not altered the story-line drastically. But to have him come back leaping for joy, or lovesick, or ambitious, or with some other emotion not at all linked with that he had as he went out would break our story-thread completely, and this we never do.

The thing to remember is that we are following the inner emotional life of the principal character, the hero. We cannot see this story-line directly. We can see only the shadows it casts, what the hero says, what he does, what happens to him. But we guide ourselves by this inner feeling and change in feeling, and where the feeling does not change over a given space of time we can drop out a great deal of his actions and thoughts. But where it does change we must tell all.

Another important detail of anatomy is the emotion-motion sequence. Typically the VP character will be handled in upbeat sequences. Sentences describing him will begin with emotional material and proceed through an active verb to an object—"Angrily he glared at the villain." But the other characters in the story, true third persons, will customarily be treated in reverse style—"The villain's eyes flashed angrily." In this last you will notice the action comes first, the verb is passive, at least to the extent that it is the villain's eyes that are doing something, and finally the emotional content, "angrily," is at the end of the sentence rather than the beginning. What this sentence says in effect is that I, the hero, looked at the villain. I saw his eyes flash. From which I judged he was angry. The integrity of the viewpoint is thus maintained, and both the VP character's feelings and actions, and those of other characters as well, in this case the villain, are observed from the single point. Whenever a story seems vague or thin, this is a detail worth checking.

At the end of the paragraphs it is good practice to point to the next actor. This is a technique one can best study in plays, motion pictures, and television. Here, always, when one actor has delivered a line or performed an action, and another actor is to speak or act next, the attention of the observer is deftly directed to the next performer before he acts.

In writing this is also necessary. Curious as it may seem, even on the printed page the reader will miss part of the meaning of a speech or action to which his attention has not previously been directed.

If the heroine has been saying something, waving her hands, and the hero says something, the reader will miss part of the hero's speech. That is unless the heroine waves her hand toward the hero, unless she whirls toward him, unless she flings out a question or accusation, so that automatically we look at him to see how he will respond.

Typically this technique is employed at the ends of paragraphs, and it looks something like this:

" 'I do not know what will become of us," Matilda said quietly, 'to have to go out into this storm . . . .' She turned toward Sam."

Now ordinarily we look at Sam (whoever he is) to see what he will do or say. We will not miss anything because Matilda has obligingly pointed for us. When Sam has his say he will do something to throw the ball back to Matilda, or whoever is to perform next, so that once again our attention is transferred. Always be sure that your reader is looking at your character before the character speaks or acts. And once again, in a million variations, the technique is simply to point.

Dialog, of course, is the principal way in which this pointing is employed, and dialog itself is a vital anatomical part of nearly every story. To ask a question is to point. Always we will look automatically at the person to whom the question is addressed, to learn his reply. Accordingly, between question and answer there will nearly always be a paragraph break. And here, as a technique to help in this business of making a story hang together, is a trick that may be useful.

You have doubtless been taught the objective style of writing which dissects a topic into sub-topics and then sets each sub-topic in a near paragraph to itself, a sort of little coffin complete with head space. But in good fiction you never write a complete paragraph.

Instead you always set either the last sentence of the paragraph as the first sentence of the next paragraph, or you pick up the first sentence of the next paragraph and make it the last sentence of the paragraph ahead.

Your reader, like yourself, has been taught to read to the end of a sense, which in objective writing is also the end of a paragraph. He has acquired this as a lifelong habit. But in good fiction when, as he is accustomed to do, he reads to the end of a paragraph, he has read all the sense of that paragraph and one sentence into the next. He has to read the first sentence of the next paragraph to complete the new subtopic, the new sense he has begun.

Here habit catches him again because he will seldom quit reading in the middle of a paragraph. So he reads to the end of the paragraph, only to find himself trapped again halfway into the sense of the next paragraph. If we use this technique properly, he will never find a spot where he feels he can quit reading until he reaches the end of the story.

Always parade your dialog in a story. It is the livest part of your tale and typically should begin paragraphs. Use the identifications of the speakers, the "he said" or "she retorted," as pegs to hold your emotional description. Say "he snarled," or "she wept," or the like, using the verbs to state the emotion. Or vary this by using motions rather than "said" and its synonyms—" 'Oh yes!' He straightened angrily. 'I don't think so.' " The action identifies the speaker, and we do not have to say that he spoke the quoted words. And above all be sure that your dialog is natural.

This you can test by having it read aloud or even by reading it aloud to yourself. Listen to it as you write it. And never, never, never have a character speak in the formal written language. Just as in German and in Latin, so also in English there is a high, formal language used for scientific papers, legal documents, and the like, written but never spoken. And there is a low English, the informal tongue we speak. Good stories are invariably written in the informal spoken language.

There remain two more techniques which are essential in viewpoint, but which are also objective in some aspects. These are *pointers* and *plants*.

Plants are simply tangible things, significant physical properties which are to be used in the story. They must be mentioned, "planted," ahead of time so that we are not unduly surprised when they are used in the scene. Thus, if we are going to produce Grandpa's pistol to shoot somebody on page 14, we must be sure to have someone open a drawer and remark idly, "Oh, here's Grandpa's old pistol," on about page 6 or 7.

Pointers are ordinarily actions or speeches implying future actions. These, too, we must be sure to supply so that no significant action in the story comes as a complete surprise; the reader must always be oriented ahead and so catch the gleam of the things to come. For example, if hero and villain are going to have a gunfight, several pages previously the reader must be told the villain is on the prowl or that the hero has buckled on his gun with a bleak premonition. We have noted already how we must point from speech to speech, paragraph to paragraph, but we must remember also to point to events still further ahead. But this usually will come without trouble as we master viewpoint.

CHAPTER IX

Revision and Selling

WHEN THE FIRST DRAFT is finished and the fine flush of subjective creation is over, then comes the brutal part of fictioneering. This is revision or surgery, an objective technique, difficult to master and yet tremendously rewarding if one takes the trouble to learn it thoroughly.

I have known several successful writers who claimed that they never revised. They had found that revision seemed to cut the life from their writings. Or so they said. Well, perhaps so. But personally I always wondered just what they meant by "not revising." I have seen too many of them who have learned to revise, very slowly and painfully, as they went along, on their first draft.

When they had finished what they called their first draft, say sixteen to twenty pages, they would have also a pile of at least a hundred discarded pages, partially written, changed, edited. It always seemed to be a laborious way to revise.

In our university classes over a period of about twenty years we have found that ordinarily it is best to drive ahead with the first draft as rapidly and continuously as possible, trying never to look back. Naturally, this method will not suit all writers, and you will need to experiment and find out for yourself which is your best way. But most of our successful selling writers seem to arrive eventually at a procedure something like this:

One. Write your first draft as rapidly and continuously as you can manage it, trying never to look back, not even to the preceding page.

Two. Now let this first draft "get cold." Set it aside for a day or two and think and do something else. At the very least, let it cool overnight, because in the morning you may have a very different idea of it than you had the night before.

Three. Now read it through coldly and jot down a very brief summary of the plot. You know what the parts of a plot are; you know where they should be. This is a surgical examination you are making now to determine whether or not the baby has the requisite number of arms and legs, a head on the right end, and feet where they should be. If you cannot synopsize the plot, condensing it into a couple of paragraphs, then you know something is the matter. And you know also just where surgery is needed.

Try to do this as cold-bloodedly as possible, just as though you were criticizing the story of some completely unknown. With your own story, as with your own child, you will never be able to be as completely objective as you might be with the work of a stranger. This, incidentally, is why surgeons never operate on members of their own family and dislike to work even on close friends. Our own are too close to us; we cannot see them clearly enough for our objective techniques. If you have a competent coach, or writer-friend who is not an amateur, perhaps here you can ask him to read for you and judge the plot. But for the most part, painfully and clumsily you must learn to do this for yourself.

Four. Now, if you deem it necessary, rewrite the story to incorporate the plot corrections needed. Start at the first, and go through from beginning to end again. Don't start at the end and work back. What we are trying to do here is not to eliminate that living, first-time-it-happened, very-first-account feeling. All too often a too-meticulous writer cuts all the life out of his story when he tries to revise. So you bear this in mind. Cut as little as possible; change as little as possible. You are trying to make the story seem more real, more believable. For goodness' sake, never change anything simply for the sake of literary style or because you think it could be "better English."

Five. You are not finished yet. Let this revision cool and go over it from beginning to end once again. This time look for minutiae. Read it one time to make sure all the paragraphs tie together. Edit with a pencil if they don't. Read it again to be sure there are no bad transitions, no pronouns with indefinite antecedents, no "he's" or "she's" that could refer to almost anybody. Read it again to see if it cannot be speeded up, if, perhaps, paragraphs or even whole sections cannot profitably be cut out. Read it once more to be sure you have introduced all the characters in the first four pages, you have planted all the properties you use, and you have pointed to all the important actions.

In brief, make about four or five versions of your story after the first draft, trying hard to concentrate on just one thing in each version. That is, one revision in which you correct the plot. Another in which you cut and trim for speed and length. Another in which you watch for details, clumsy sentences, bad transitions, indefinite pronouns, excess wordage, and the like.

This infinitely tedious business is what polishing a story amounts to, and it is why the yarns in the great national magazines are called "slick" stories. For the most part they are just that—tales the author has done over and over and over, with infinite pains, just as he might polish a precious stone.

I admit sadly, only too often the ultimate result seems to be a brilliant polish job with absolutely nothing underneath it, not even a piece of glass. But nevertheless, it is what most magazine editors, and nearly all book editors as well, have come to expect.

There is a difference between a first-draft story, however vital, and a laboriously polished "slick" story, just as there is between a diamond in the rough and a finely cut and polished gem. The editors, objectively minded for the most part, all too often can see only the objective polish. They are ordinarily quite unable to recognize a diamond in the rough. Which is why you find so much pastry in popular print; and conversely why it is often so extraordinarily difficult to market a truly brilliant original story.

The popular-market editors are not looking for enduring literature. Instead, like the carnival salesmen, they seek merchandise with flash and glitter, something to catch the eye with instant appeal, however temporary and tawdry that flash may be.

This is not to criticise the "slick" merchants. They are highly competent merchandisers, supplying a definite demand. It is as profitable, and as honest, to learn to satisfy these buyers as it would be to produce a glossier polish for automobiles or a more colorful finish for fingernails. But in the "slick" sense used here it is not literature we are trying to produce. Instead, this is simply a commercial product of our times, a high-gloss style. Once you have mastered it, you may find it is exceedingly profitable. But it is a commercial process, not art.

You can learn a very great deal about it by studying the published stories in slick fiction-books and magazines, by deliberately matching your style with that of the published examples, and by picking up all of the usable tricks of the trade you find on the published page. As with men's clothing styles, only a very little originality is desired in these stories. They are not supposed to have depth; nor even make the reader think. Alas, some of them do not even keep him awake either. But that perhaps is another story.

The revision of a serious literary work is another matter. Do not let yourself be deceived here by the fact that a great deal of trash in the modern market is blatantly termed "literary." Fiction writing is at the lowest ebb of a century in our day, and it is highly doubtful if any of our so-called great writers will be remembered at all a century hence. But if you are writing "with a purpose"—and believe me this is quite without profit or honor in our age—then you must also learn to revise something in the above manner, but with far more underlying purpose. Your primary consideration here is to bring out your theme.

No one can tell you just what words to put down or the order to put them in to convey the message, which may not be in succinct words even in your own conscious mind. But there is one guiding principle, much neglected in modern education, which has held true for thousands of years.

That is that the immortal story is a song, it has music as well as words, it is in the spoken, and not the written, language. For serious literary revision, it is good practice to read constantly aloud to yourself, listening to the rhythm and tune of your words. Or have someone else read to you, or read it onto a tape recorder and play it back so that you may hear it. For as St. Paul said it long ago, "Faith cometh by hearing." Christ also said, "The kingdom of God cometh not with observation." And our primary problem here is to make the reader hear what he sees.

If we can, that is, beat the rhythm of our feelings into his subconscious, amoeba mind, we have captured our reader forever, and he will never forget. The ages of great literature have also been ages of great poets. We have none in our day—not one who speaks from the heart. But perhaps a better time will come. Perhaps even now in some garret some writer is slowly, painfully revising, listening for the music of his words, for the song that surpasses understanding. For this sort of revision, the most difficult of all, I have no precepts save this one already given. With Homer, as with Milton and Whitman, the song is mostly to the singer, and returneth to him, and no one else can say positively just which note he should sing. But when he does sing it, his own ear will know.

In pulp-fiction markets, stories are ordinarily first draft with only minor revisions, a page here and there corrected. On the opposite extreme, students and graduates of our writing classes have done as many as fifteen revisions of a story before having it acepted by top-flight national magazines. Three or four revisions of a novel are quite commonplace. And perhaps it is worth while to add here a final caution about the great national magazines and many of the book publishers.

Typically, they are quite cautious about asking for revision. They seem to fear that an author will consider a request for a rewrite as an acceptance of his story. So, when they reject a manuscript, the writer needs to know how to read between the lines of the refusal and how to judge whether he should attempt a revision and resubmission to the same market or instead send the story on to someone else.

A flat, formal, rejection, slip, or a form letter of refusal, saying, "this does not fit into our current plans," or, "we simply cannot work up enough enthusiasm," of course offers no encouragement. Try your story somewhere else. But if the letter of rejection is specific in its complaints, that is another matter altogether.

If, for instance, the rejection says, "this is too long," or, "our readers objected to the hero killing the villain and the heroine, too," or, "the climax seems to lack impact," or the like, why these are tacit invitations to revise and resubmit. In the top-flight editorial houses, it is common practice for a manuscript to go back and forth between author and editor three, four, and five times before finally it is accepted.

For my part, I have my doubts about the worth of this business. All too often it has seemed to me that the fifth revision, "completely acceptable," is suspiciously like a facsimile of the very first version which the editor has conveniently forgotten in the meantime and now thinks is just what he was striving to achieve. The moral here is, never throw away your first version. For this happens, and it is something a writer must learn to expect in an objective, plural-minded world which considers six copies six times more valuable than one.

To repeat, always read your rejection again; read it a day or so later just to be sure you have not ignored a tacit invitation to resubmit. Almost always, positive criticisms of a story are bids for changes which may bring acceptances.

Working in white fury, the genius may produce excellence in first draft. But most of us are not geniuses. Most of us have to learn, very slowly and painfully, how to write at all. Most of us would profit if we took even more pains to learn how to rewrite, to revise.

Almost without exception the modern successful short story, novelette, or novel is a painful revision. The easier it seems to read, the more laborious and painful you can be sure it was to rewrite. Yet once again:

To learn to revise, to cut, and rewrite is the most profitable technique a writer can master. It may not convert his production into great literature. But it may very easily bring him ten times the financial return he would have received from his unpolished first drafts.

Now for the actual physical form of the completed manuscript, ready for presentation to the editor; and we are about done with anatomy. The story should be legibly typewritten on good-stock paper, 8½×11 inches, on one side of the paper only. And—do I need to say it?—always keep a carbon.

On page one, put your name and address in the extreme upper left-hand corner. Put the word-count in the upper right-hand corner, counting in round numbers. Thus: "App. 2,000 words" or 2,500, or 5,000, or whatever. Never give "2,162¼," or any such ultra-precision. Here, also, if you are offering only certain rights, you say so under the word-count—"First serial rights, only," or the like. But usually, until one is an established writer, the editor will buy what he pleases, and it is well to let the matter of rights go until later.

About a third of the way down from the top, center your title in capital letters. Below this, center your name or pen name, if you are using one.

Then give yourself about an inch and a half more of white space and begin your story. Leave at least a one-inch margin all around, and an inch and a half to the left is even better. Put a small pencil-mark near the bottom of your page to guide you so that there will be a bottom margin also.

On succeeding pages, leave about an inch and a half of margin at the top. Put either your name or the title of the story in the extreme upper right-hand corner, followed by about three dashes and the page number.

At the bottom of the last page, repeat your name and address so that if, by some chance, the first page is lost, the manuscript can still be identified.

Do not bind your manuscript permanently. A neat folder or cover to hold the manuscript helps in sales appearance, but it is not necessary. Mail manuscripts flat, using a 10×13 kraft envelope, and a $9\frac{1}{2} \times 12\frac{1}{2}$ return envelope to slide flat inside. Be sure to attach sufficient postage to both envelopes, if you want your story considered. Do not send loose stamps.

Larger manuscripts can be sent by express, if desired, and the express company will obligingly collect return carrying charges from you. Large manuscripts are nearly always submitted unbound. Use a stout stationery box, and it is good practice to put your name and address on the box also, as well as on the manuscript.

Addresses of editors can be obtained from their publications or from the various market lists published for writers. Both the *Writers' Digest* and *Author and Journalist* publish very good market lists, and there are also several very complete market guides available in book form.

Keep a record of where you sent your stories and of postage used, since this is a deductible expense. Stationery, typewriter ribbons and repair, books and magazines used in research, and even a portion of the expense of your household, if you use your house as an office, are usually deductible, also. Ask your income-tax man about all this when you prepare your next return. He can probably save you quite a tidy sum.

One last bit of advice and we are done. I do not know where the bump of persistence is located in the anatomy of story or story writers. But I am certain it is the most important part of their make-up. A story that will hold together through enough mailings to sell is a rare blessing, and a story writer who will persist until he sells his product is the rarest of the rare.

And yet no quality is more rewarding. I have known stories to sell on their fifty-first trip out. I have known them to sell on their third submission to the same editor—yes, that is possible, although it is better to be cautious about repeated submissions. I have listened to authors of tremendous best sellers tell me of editors by the dozen who rejected their work. And I have long since become convinced that there is a market somewhere for any kind of writing, if one is willing to look long enough.

So never, never give up! "In the beginning was the Word," so the Bible says, and in the end, I think, will be the *word*, also.

I hope it will be a word, or maybe words, *you* thought up and put down and sold, your own creation.

119

Date Due